TEELINE
GOLD STANDARD
FOR JOURNALISTS

From beginner to 100 wpm with essential
speed building and exam practice

Marie Cartwright

CD-ROM inside

www.pearsonschools.co.uk
✓ Free online support
✓ Useful weblinks
✓ 24 hour online ordering

0845 630 44 44

Part of Pearson

Heinemann is an imprint of Pearson Education Limited, a company incorporated in England and Wales, having its registered office at Edinburgh Gate, Harlow, Essex, CM20 2JE. Registered company number: 872828

www.pearsonschoolsandfecolleges.co.uk

Heinemann is a registered trademark of Pearson Education Limited

Text © Pearson Education Limited 2009

First published 2009

2023
22

British Library Cataloguing in Publication Data
A catalogue record for this book is available from the British Library

ISBN 978 0 435471 71 2

Copyright notice
All rights reserved. No part of this publication may be reproduced in any form or by any means (including photocopying or storing it in any medium by electronic means and whether or not transiently or incidentally to some other use of this publication) without the written permission of the copyright owner, except in accordance with the provisions of the Copyright, Designs and Patents Act 1988 or under the terms of a licence issued by the Copyright Licensing Agency, Saffron House, 6–10 Kirby Street, London EC1N 8TS (www.cla.co.uk). Applications for the copyright owner's written permission should be addressed to the publisher.

Edited by Liz Cartmell
Typeset by Saxon Graphics Ltd, Derby
Cover photos JUPITERIMAGES/ Comstock Premium/ Alamy (main image); INSADCO Photography/ Alamy/Alamy (background)
Text © Marie Cartwright and the NCTJ
Teeline outlines © The Teeline Partnership
Examination materials © NCTJ
Printed in the UK by Ashford Colour Press Ltd

Acknowledgements
I would like to thank my very experienced colleague, Anne Atkins, for checking the Teeline outlines; Allan Colley for his superb technical assistance with the recording of the dictation passages; and students on past NCTJ courses at Norton College, Sheffield, for their very positive comments and feedback on the theory section of the book.

I would also like to thank my husband, Steve, for his support and encouragement over the past year while I have been writing and recording and for his patience and help with checking.

Marie Cartwright

Foreword

If I had a pound for every journalism trainee who has moaned about shorthand, I could retire today. And if I had a second pound for every editor who has told me just how important shorthand is, I'd be retiring a rich man.

I guess it's possible that, somewhere, there's a cub reporter who loves learning shorthand and looks forward to every lesson. I doubt it. I've seen more enthusiasm from my children for extra maths. But I've also seen the rising confidence of journalists who take the trouble to develop a good shorthand note.

These days we carry all the digital recording equipment we could wish for, yet we need shorthand as much as ever. It's a journalistic skill of great value, as useful for the internet and broadcast journalist as it has always been for the newspaper reporter.

I think there are three reasons why it remains so important. The first is practical. A good shorthand note is an accurate record of a conversation and will be accepted as such in a court of law. Talk to someone for an hour with a digital recorder and it will take an hour to play it back. Not so with a shorthand note, from which it is easy to extract important quotes. As for court reporting, try taking out a recorder and see how that goes down with the judge.

The second reason is that taking a shorthand note makes you concentrate. You listen carefully to what's being said. It's good when journalists listen carefully.

Thirdly, shorthand betokens seriousness, commitment to the craft, and care about detail. As the written word proliferates with the expansion of the internet, we hope that discerning readers will look for words they can trust. In learning shorthand, journalists demonstrate their belief in core values such as accuracy.

But don't take my word for it. Ask editors – online, broadcast, print – what they are looking for when they recruit. Ask whether they still see value in shorthand. Their answers should give you every encouragement to learn it.

The truth is, joy in shorthand comes with mastering it. This excellent book will help you do just that.

Kim Fletcher
Chairman
National Council for the Training of Journalists

Contents

Introduction

Part 1

Revision exercises 96

Drill exercises – special outlines/common words 113

Part 2

Part 3

Introduction

Teeline shorthand was invented in the 1960s by the late James Hill. Unlike some other shorthand systems, Teeline is linked to ordinary handwriting and has a degree of flexibility. It is based on the alphabet and is simple, logical and easy to learn.

The NCTJ link

The National Council for the Training of Journalists (NCTJ) was founded in 1951 as an organisation to oversee the training of journalists for the newspaper industry. Today it delivers the premier training scheme in the UK and plays an influential role in all areas of journalism education and training.

The importance of shorthand for journalists

Shorthand is an essential skill for journalists and an accurate and reliable shorthand note is a vital requirement of the job. Editors have high standards and many will only employ trainees who have achieved 100 words per minute (wpm). Once employed, trainees are encouraged to work towards the National Certificate Examination (NCE) and one of the entry requirements for this examination is the NCTJ's 100 wpm shorthand qualification.

People are often surprised that shorthand in a digital age remains such a vital skill. In fact, shorthand is now a more important skill than it ever has been, as journalists are increasingly working under greater time pressures and are expected to publish news and information 24 hours a day. Journalists simply don't have time to rewind a tape recorder and transcribe a long interview.

Although the learning process can be protracted and painstaking, there is no better method than shorthand to enable you to get all the facts and quotes you need to be a truly professional journalist.

In a recent survey of more than 200 editors, the overwhelming conclusion was that there should be no surrender for the need to have an adequate shorthand note. This research also concluded that traditional skills, which included finding stories, writing news and media law as well as shorthand, were more important than the new skills of video production, podcasts, blogs and search engine optimisation.

In this age of converging journalism skills, with the traditional boundaries between broadcast and print news delivery blurred by the online publishing revolution, these core traditional skills remain the bedrock of quality journalism.

Examinations

NCTJ shorthand examinations are available at approved centres at speeds of 60–120 wpm. Details can be found on the NCTJ website: www.nctj.com. Remember though, not only are you aiming for success in the examination, but also credibility in the workplace. Journalists may be required to present their shorthand notes as evidence in a court of law so it is imperative that the note is accurate and reliable.

How to work through this book

It is important that you work through this book in the order in which it is presented. An accompanying CD is provided so that you can practise your Teeline from the spoken word as well as from the written word. Dictation passages contained on the CD will be indicated by the symbol 💿

Teeline is a flexible shorthand system and there may be several different ways to write a word, each one equally correct. However, while you are learning Teeline, it is better to follow the examples shown in this book. When you have a thorough knowledge and understanding of the system, you can modify it to suit your own needs if you wish.

Part 1 Learning the theory and introduction to dictation

This part of the book will focus mainly on learning the theory. Short sentences and graded dictation will be introduced early on. Shorthand and longhand keys are provided at the back of the book.

Each dictation passage will be for 1 minute, rising progressively to 1½ minutes towards the end of the theory section. Short timings will allow you to not only develop your listening and memorising techniques, but also to focus on the quality of your note. It is important that your shorthand notes are neat and of a good quality so that you are able to read them accurately and without hesitation. Dictation will start at 40 wpm and will be repeated at 50 wpm and then 60 wpm.

Revision exercises and drill exercises are added to the end of the theory section. These are very useful for checking knowledge and identifying any areas of weakness. It is a good idea to work through these exercises after the appropriate units of theory have been covered so that you may address any areas of weakness as you progress. Alternatively, you may return to these as a means of revision as you are working through the speed development passages.

Part 2 Speed development

Part 2 will introduce 2-minute dictation passages from 50 wpm to 100 wpm, each passage being repeated at two higher speeds. These will be preceded by selected words to practise before starting the dictation. The majority of these passages have been taken from past NCTJ shorthand examinations and will give you a taste of exam style dictation and content. The matching shorthand will accompany each passage.

Part 3 Examination practice

This section provides guidance on how to prepare for examinations. Sample examination passages with accompanying dictation at speeds of 60 wpm – 120 wpm are available on NCTJ's website, www.nctj.com

Getting started

Equipment/materials required

You will need:

- a spiral-bound, good-quality, ruled notebook in which to write your shorthand
- a pen or pencil (choose a fine-nib pen or a good-quality, sharp HB pencil)
- a CD player or a computer with Windows Media Player (or equivalent).

Use of notebook

You should rule a left-hand margin of 2–3 cm on each page. This can be used for corrections in the classroom or for such things as the longhand spelling of names or places, telephone numbers or follow-up information in the workplace.

Work through the notebook one way and when you reach the end, turn it round and work back to the front. A rubber band is useful to secure the used pages.

Write the date each day at the bottom of the page. This makes it easy to find notes and information. Also, write the date you start using your notebook and the date you finish using it on the front cover along with your name and a contact telephone number (in case you mislay it). Keep used notebooks in a safe place as they may be required at a later date.

Teeline may be written with a pen or pencil. Try both before deciding which one you prefer. Whichever you choose, always have a spare to hand when taking dictation.

Practice routine

Teeline is a skill and, as with any skill, it requires regular practice if you want to improve and progress. It is far more beneficial to practise for a short time every day than for one long period once or twice a week.

If you require additional dictation practice, speed development CDs are available for purchase from the NCTJ.

Introducing Teeline

The Teeline shorthand system is based on the alphabet that we are already familiar with, but in order to write faster than normal writing, letters are reduced and streamlined.

Teeline letters take the same positions as regular letters of the alphabet, i.e. **G**, **J**, **P** and **Q** cut the line, **T** is written above the line (the horizontal stroke) and the other letters sit on the line. Vowels have two forms – full vowels and indicators. Vowels are written smaller than consonants – about one-third the size of consonants.

If your handwriting is small, your Teeline will probably be small and if your handwriting is large, your Teeline will probably be large. This is quite acceptable, but it is important to keep the letters in good proportion to one another and to write them as neatly as you can. Teeline letters are called '**outlines**'.

The Teeline alphabet

	Teeline letter	Vowel indicator	Writing explanation
A			The full vowel is the top part of capital **A**. The indicator is either the downstroke or the upstroke.
B			A streamlined
C			Same as lower case **C**. Also represents **CK** in words, e.g. lu**ck**.
D			A short dash written on the line.
E			The full vowel is the bottom part of capital **E**. The indicator is either the downstroke or the horizontal stroke.
F	or		Part of a handwritten Also used for words with the sound of **F**, e.g. enou**gh**, **ph**one.
G			A streamlined form of Also used for words with the sound of **DGE**, e.g. le**dge**, nu**dge**.

	Teeline letter	Vowel indicator	Writing explanation
H			The downstroke of capital **H**.
I			A handwritten _i_ but with a sharp angle. The dot is omitted. The indicator is either the downstroke or the upstroke.
J			A streamlined _j_ without the dot.
K			Capital **K** with the side downstroke removed.
L			The downstroke of a handwritten _l_ with a curl. Can also be streamlined and written either upwards or downwards.
M			A streamlined handwritten _m_ with a single curve.
N			The hook and downstroke of a handwritten _n_.
O			The full vowel is only used occasionally. The indicator is the shallow under-section written from left to right.
P			The downstroke of lower case **P**. Written through the line when it begins a word. Same size as **H**.
Q			The loop which joins **Q** to **U** in handwriting _qu_. Written through the line.
R			The first stroke of the old cursive handwritten **R**. Always written upwards.
S			A small circle taken from a handwritten _s_. Can be written in the most convenient direction.
T			Taken from the horizontal stroke of **T/t**. When standing alone or preceded by a vowel or letter **S**, it is written above the writing line (to distinguish it from **D**). This is known as the **T** position.

	Teeline letter	Vowel indicator	Writing explanation
U			The full vowel is a small, narrow version of capital **U**. The indicator is reduced to one side downstroke. Same as indicator **E** but cannot be confused in context.
V			The same as a lower case **V**. Written upright with a sharp angle so as not to confuse with full vowel **I**.
W			A streamlined handwritten ...ᴡ...with a single curve.
X			The same as a printed **X**. Usually it is better if ...ᴨ.. is written first.
Y			The same as a handwritten ..y...with the tail removed.
Z			Taken from old-style handwritten ..ᵹ..... Write Teeline letter **S** with a small curled tail.

Exercise 1.1

Copy the letters of the alphabet **A–M** neatly and accurately. Make sure you follow the direction of writing as indicated by the arrows. Say the letters as you write them and this will help you to remember them. A good way to memorise letters or words is to **drill** them.

Drilling is a means of learning by repetition. Each letter (or word) should be written in longhand in the margin and a neat Teeline outline for that letter (or word) written next to it. Write one letter (or word) per line down the page. Then write the outlines as many times as you need to in this way until you can write them accurately and without hesitation.

Exercise 1.2

Copy the letters of the alphabet **N–Z** neatly and accurately and then drill them until you can write them without hesitation.

Common words represented by letters of the alphabet

Some commonly occurring words can be shortened to make writing even quicker. They should be practised regularly so that you are able to write them quickly and without hesitation.

A	....∧........	able, able to, ability, after
	......\........	a
	....\......	at (written in the **T** position)
B	......6........	be, been
C	.....c........	once, offence
D	..........─......	do, day
E	....L........	electric
	.....L⸗.......	England (two small sloping dashes, written upwards under an outline indicate a capital letter)
	......l........	ever, every
F	.....ℓ........	from
G	.....?........	go, gentleman
H	......l.......	he
I	.....ʎ........	I, eye
K	.....<.......	kind, like, knowledge
L	.....ℓ........	letter, local
M	....⌢........	me
	...........⌢......	time (written in the **T** position)
N	......ʌ........	and
	......η.......	begin, began, begun (written hanging from the line)
O	....	of (written in the **T** position)
P	.....│........	pence, page, police
Q	.....ʋ.......	question, equal
R	.............╱.....	are
S	.....o........	south, southern
T	.....─.........	to (written in the **T** position)
U	......ʋ........	you

V	.....V........	very, have, village, versus
	.....v........	evidence, evident (written hanging from the line)
W	.....⌣.......	we
X	.....X.......	accident
Y	.....Ɯ.......	your

Exercise 1.3

Copy the common words represented by letters **A–M** and then drill them until you can write them without hesitation.

Exercise 1.4

Transcribe the following common words represented by letters **A–M**:

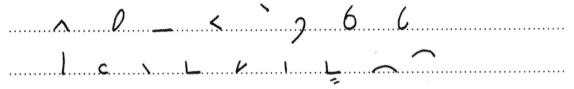

Exercise 1.5

Copy the common words represented by letters **N–Y** and then drill them until you can write them without hesitation.

Exercise 1.6

Transcribe the following common words represented by letters **N–Y**:

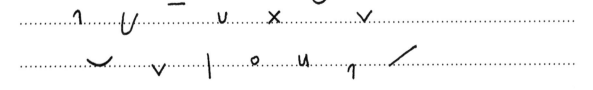

Always check your work with the keys at the back of the book and make any necessary corrections.

Joining letters

Teeline letters are joined together to form words, just as they are in ordinary handwriting. They are generally written in one smooth movement without lifting the pen/pencil from the page. Practise writing the following outlines:

| in | if | it | am | an | as |

Unit 2
Writing in Teeline

Teeline follows ordinary spelling, although occasionally phonetics (sounds) are used if helpful. In order to write words quickly, all unnecessary letters are removed and only the **skeleton** of a word is written.

For example, in the following short sentence all unnecessary consonants and vowels have been removed, but it is still easy to read.

Thr r sm jbs fr wch shrthnd is ncsry.

When words are reduced, the resulting skeleton could occasionally represent more than one word, but the sense of the sentence **(context)** will make it clear which word is required. The above sentence written in full would be: There are some jobs for which shorthand is necessary.

Vowels which **must** be written are those at the **beginning of words** and those **sounded at the end of words**. For example:

| am | in | if | no | so | era |

Removal of unnecessary letters

1. Remove vowels in the middle of words

pear	becomes	pr
hair	becomes	hr
rib	becomes	rb
quit	becomes	qt

Sometimes it is easier to write a word by leaving in a medial vowel.

For example, when **B** is followed by **G** or **N**.

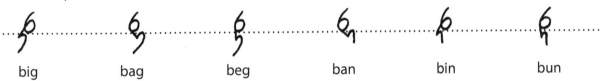

| big | bag | beg | ban | bin | bun |

2. Remove silent letters

dumb	becomes	dm	
cave	becomes	cv	
light	becomes	lt	
hedge	becomes	hg	

3. Remove one of double letters

ball	becomes	bl	
odd	becomes	od	
little	becomes	ltl	
dull	becomes	dl	

Exercise 2.1

Read the following sentences from which all unnecessary letters have been removed.

1. Tln is fn t lrn.
2. Rglr prctc is ndd if u wnt t rch th stndrd rqrd.
3. Rprtrs nd t b abl t rt fst n acrt Tln.
4. Shrthnd is an imprtnt skl fr a jrnlst.
5. Prctc mks prfct.

Position of writing

At the beginning of a word the first letter is usually written in its normal position and then the other letters in the word just follow on. However, when a word starts with a small letter or a vowel which is followed by a longer letter, it is better to write the second letter in its normal writing position so that the outline does not drop too far below the writing line. When letter **K** follows **H**, **J** or **P**, it is better to write **K** on the side. For example:

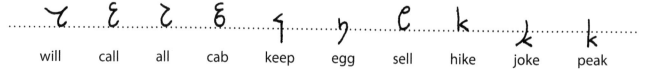

will   call   all   cab   keep   egg   sell   hike   joke   peak

Exercise 2.2

Remove all unnecessary letters from the following words and write the Teeline outlines:

made   deal   call   dove   will   jam   tough   rule   wave

Exercise 2.3

Read and copy the following Teeline letters. Can you suggest words for them?

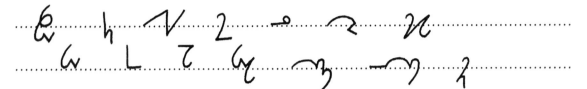

Punctuation

Punctuation marks are not generally used when writing Teeline. However, it is important to use a full stop to enable accurate reading of notes.

A Teeline full stop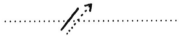

a sloping line written upwards through the writing line

All other punctuation marks are the same as in longhand, but the following may be useful:

dash   hyphen   paragraph

A capital letter is indicated by two small sloping dashes, written upwards, underneath an outline, for example:

Spain   David   Teeline

Exercise 2.4

Read the following sentences and then copy them neatly and accurately, saying the words as you write them.

1. ....

2. ....

3. ....

4. ....

5. ....

6. ....

7. ....

8. ....

9. ....

10. ....

Unit 3
Additional Teeline characters

As well as the Teeline alphabet, there are additional characters which are used to represent letter combinations.

CH ....🎵...... **C** is joined to **H**. It starts in the **T** position so that **H** is written on the writing line (the normal position of letter **H**).

If a word does not start with **CH**, then it just follows on from the previous letter.

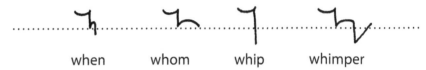

| cheer | church | teacher | patch |

WH ....🎵..... **W** is joined to **H**. It starts in the **T** position so that **H** is written on the writing line in its normal position.

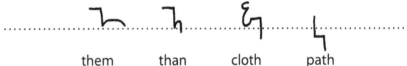

| when | whom | whip | whimper |

TH ....🎵...... **T** is joined to **H**. **T** is written in its normal position and **H** just follows on so that it is written in its normal position on the writing line.

If a word does not start with **TH**, then it just follows on from the previous letter.

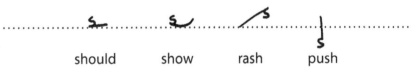

| them | than | cloth | path |

SH ....S...... The letter **S** is used to represent **SH**.

| should | show | rash | push |

Exercise 3.1

Read and copy the following words.

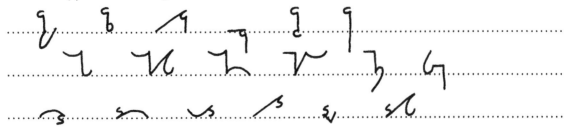

Vowels

Vowels have two forms – full vowels and indicators:

	Full vowel	Indicators
A	..⋀......	..../....... *and* .....＼.....
E	...⌐.....	....⎸....... *and* ...._.....
I	..../.....	...../..... *and* ...../.....
O	...ᵒ......	..........⌄..............
U	...ᴜ......	..............⎸..............

Vowels are written smaller than consonants, about one third the size. The vowel indicator is more commonly used than the full vowel.

As explained in Unit 2, a vowel is always written when it starts a word and when it is sounded at the end of a word:

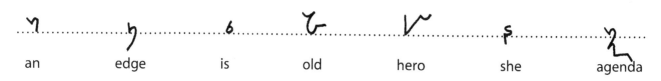

an	edge	is	old	hero	she	agenda

When a word begins or ends with a double vowel, either the first or the more strongly sounded vowel is written:

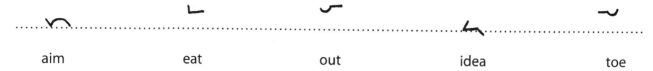

aim	eat	out	idea	toe

If there is likely to be any confusion when reading back, a vowel may be written next to the outline. However, this is rarely necessary as the context of the sentence usually suggests the correct word. For heavy sounds use a full vowel and for light sounds use an indicator:

ship	shop	shape	sheep

Special outlines

Frequently used words can be reduced to make writing even quicker. We already use many longhand abbreviated words, for example:

company	(co.)	...ᵔ.....	etcetera	(etc.)	...ᵗ.......
representative	(rep.)	...ᒣ....	account	(a/c)	....ᵹ......

Special outlines should be learned as they occur in each unit. Very often only the beginning of a word is written and it is just not finished off. A good way to learn special outlines is to drill them.

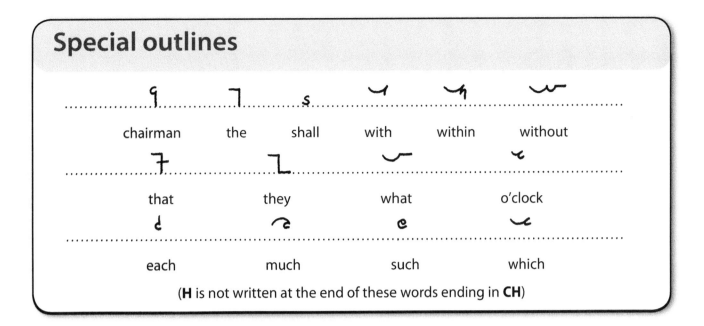

chairman	the	shall	with	within	without

that	they	what	o'clock

each	much	such	which

(**H** is not written at the end of these words ending in **CH**)

Dictation practice

There are two useful ways to practise writing from dictation in the early stages of learning.

Method 1

Read the sentences and then copy the outlines neatly and accurately into your notebook, writing on every third line. This will give you two blank lines underneath on which to practise. Listen to the dictation and write the sentences on the first blank line. If you cannot remember how to write a word, glance at the line above and copy the outline. Repeat this exercise by writing on the second blank line and then try it a third time with no guide in front of you.

Method 2

Another useful way to practise is by shadow writing (sometimes called ghost writing or dry penning). Read the sentences and then when listening to the dictation write over the top of the outlines with a retracted pen. Do this as many times as you need to until you feel confident about taking down the dictation without a guide.

Exercise 3.2

Read the following sentences and then prepare them for dictation using one of the methods described above.

1.

2.

3.

4.

5.

Unit 4
Letter S

Letter **S** is a small circle and can be written either clockwise or anti-clockwise. It is written first if it comes at the beginning of a word and last if it comes at the end.

There are two simple rules – it goes inside curves and outside angles.

1. **S** is always written **inside** curves:

| was | sell | sobs | seems | museum | sugar | soon | swims |

S is written **inside** the curve if it comes between a straight letter and a curve:

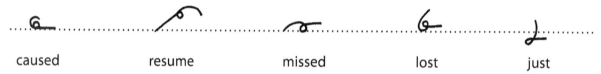

| caused | resume | missed | lost | just |

2. **S** is always written on the **outside** angle of two straight letters:

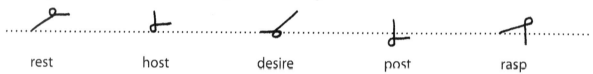

| rest | host | desire | post | rasp |

S can be written either side of a straight letter, but generally it is better to write it in an anti-clockwise direction in order to keep the straight letter straight. Practise both ways then choose the way you prefer and keep to it:

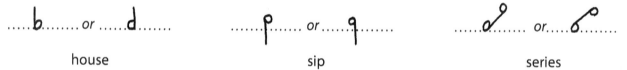

| house | sip | series |

S and Z

When **Z** starts a word use a **Z**:

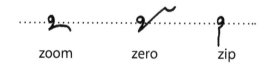

| zoom | zero | zip |

When **Z** occurs in the **middle** or the **end** of a word, use letter **S** as it is easier to write:

| razor | magazine |

S vowel S

When **S vowel S** occurs at the **beginning** or in the **middle** of a word, the vowel should be written:

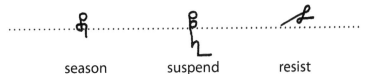

season   suspend   resist

Words which **end** in **S vowel S** can be written using a disjoined circle **S**. It is written close to the first part of the outline:

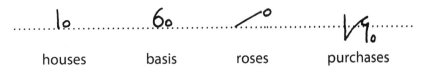

houses   basis   roses   purchases

Special outlines

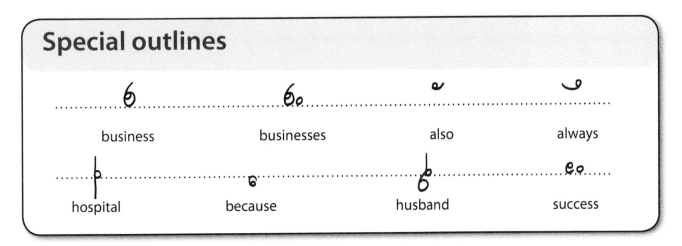

business   businesses   also   always

hospital   because   husband   success

Distinguishing outlines

When two or more frequently occurring words have the same outline, it is necessary to write each one differently in order to avoid possible errors in transcription:

his		**H** slopes in the direction of indicator **I**
has		**H** slopes in the direction of indicator **A**
this		**H** slopes in the direction of indicator **I**
these		**H** remains straight, in the direction of indicator **E**
those		**H** remains straight and indicator **O** is included
purpose		**P** remains straight
perhaps		the second **P** is sloped in the direction of indicator **A**
amaze		amuse

Exercise 4.1

Read the following sentences and then prepare them for dictation using one of the methods described earlier.

1. ....

2. ....

3. ....

4. ....

5. ....

Unit 5
Letters T and D

When writing letters **T** and **D**, a simple rule to remember is **T** – **T**op, **D** – **D**own.

Letter **T** should be written above the line in the **T position** when standing alone, beginning a word or when preceded by an **S** or a vowel:

take	tell	atom	item	sit	stab

Letter **D** should be written on the writing line when standing alone, beginning a word or when preceded by an **S** or a vowel:

dove	dam	add	idol	odd	sad

When **T** is followed by **P** or **G**, write the **T** a little lower than usual so that the **P** or **G** keeps its normal writing position through the line:

top	stop	tiger	stag	stagger

When letter **B** is followed by **T** or **D**, write the **T** at the **T**op of the circle and **D** **D**own at the bottom of the circle:

but	bottom	rabbit	bad	robbed	buds

When **T** or **D** ends a word, if possible write the whole of the outline either in the **T** or the **D** position:

sent	send	mist	missed	out	odd	net	need

Letters **T** and **D** are never joined. The first letter is written in its normal writing position and the next letter is written slightly above (**T**op) or below (**D**own) and to the right:

T followed by T

tight	total	tooth

T followed by D

tied	quoted	waited

D followed by T

date	detail	death	dated

D followed by D

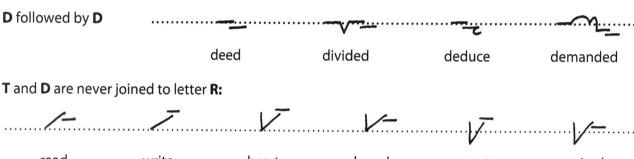

deed divided deduce demanded

T and D are never joined to letter R:

read write heart heard part paired

Exercise 5.1

Read and write the following sentences.

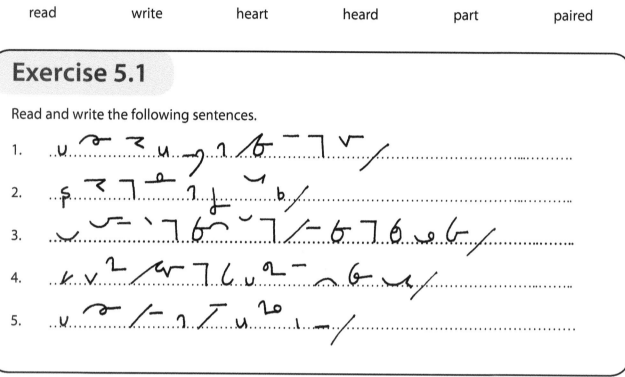

1.
2.
3.
4.
5.

F joined to T and D

Letter **F** may be written upwards or downwards

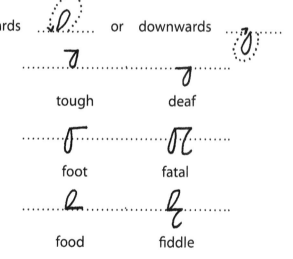

T and D start in their usual
position when followed by **F**

tough deaf

F is written downwards before **T**
(so that **T** takes its usual position, **T**op)

foot fatal

F is written upwards before **D**
(so that **D** takes its usual position, **D**own)

food fiddle

K followed by T or D

T and D should be disjoined from **K**
and written in the **T** or **D** position:

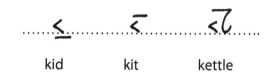

kid kit kettle

NCTJ Teeline Gold Standard for Journalists

C and K

C may be written instead of **K** in the middle
or at the end of a word to give a better outline:

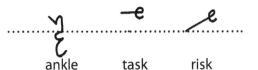

ankle   task   risk

CT and CD

When **T**, **D** or **R** follow **C**, the letters are blended together and written in one movement to make a smooth join:

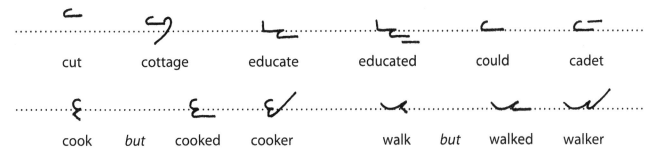

cut   cottage   educate   educated   could   cadet

cook   *but*   cooked   cooker   walk   *but*   walked   walker

Special outlines

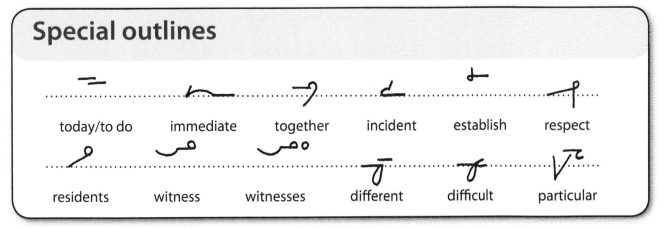

today/to do   immediate   together   incident   establish   respect

residents   witness   witnesses   different   difficult   particular

Exercise 5.2

Read and write the following sentences.

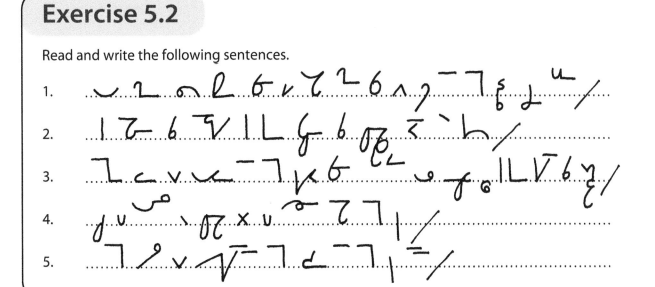

1.

2.

3.

4.

5.

Word groupings

Time can be saved if common words are joined together. These are known as **word groupings**. The first word is written in its normal position and then the rest of the outline(s) just follows on. A lot of common words can be joined together and below are a few examples of commonly used word groupings:

we shall	I shall	you will	I must	we will	to see	to say

do you	you do	that was	you are	are you	of course

we have	you have	I will have	we should have	that was a

You may **leave out** or **add** letters within a word grouping:

I **a**m sure	as **s**oon as	**we** are	it **is**	th**ey** are	wi**ll** be

tha**t** these	tha**t** those	tha**t** this	*but* that his	as **soon as possible***

*High-speed word grouping, taken from the abbreviation **asap**

ABLE or ABLE TO

A disjoined full vowel **A** is written close to the previous part of the outline:

I am able to	we are able to	he is able to	are you able to

BE or BEEN

Letter **B** 6 or just the circle of letter **B** can be used:

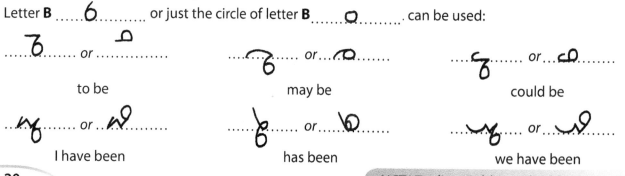

to be	may be	could be

I have been	has been	we have been

THE

The word **the** may be reduced to Teeline letter **H** when joined to other words, but the full outline should be used at the beginning of a word grouping or where it will make the word grouping easier to write and clearer to read:

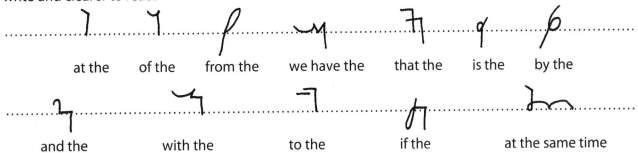

at the	of the	from the	we have the	that the	is the	by the

and the	with the	to the	if the	at the same time

FACT

The word **fact** may be reduced to **CT**:

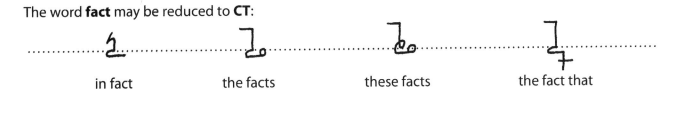

in fact	the facts	these facts	the fact that

WOULD

The word **would** is written in full when it stands alone or starts a word grouping:

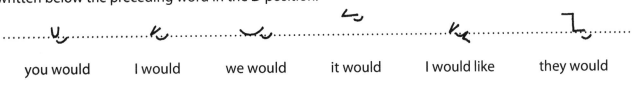

would you	would be	would have	would we	would we be able to

When **would** follows another word, it may be reduced to a small letter **W** (about half the normal size) written below the preceding word in the **D** position:

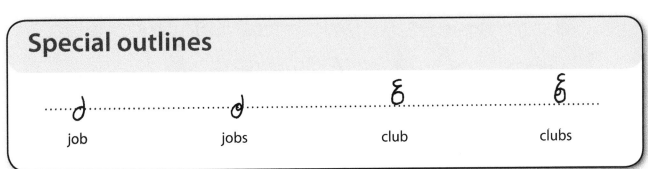

you would	I would	we would	it would	I would like	they would

Special outlines

job	jobs	club	clubs

Exercise 6.1

Read and write the following sentences.

1. _[shorthand outlines]_

2. _[shorthand outlines]_

3. _[shorthand outlines]_

4. _[shorthand outlines]_

5. _[shorthand outlines]_

Dictation passages

All the dictation passages are on the CD which accompanies this book.

When practising timed dictation passages, the following guidelines may be helpful:

1. Read the shorthand.

2. Drill any outlines which you think may cause you difficulty.

3. Start the dictation and do not stop the recording until the passage ends. If necessary, leave gaps if you fall behind or if you cannot write a word.

4. Transcribe your notes.

5. Check your shorthand and your transcription with the key.

6. Drill any outlines which caused you to hesitate or any outlines you missed out or got wrong.

7. Repeat the passage until you can take it down accurately, then try it at the higher speeds.

Exercise 6.2

Prepare the following passage for dictation.

A visit to the park

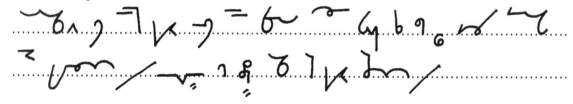

Exercise 6.3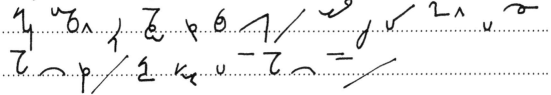

Prepare the following passage for dictation.

New job as business representative

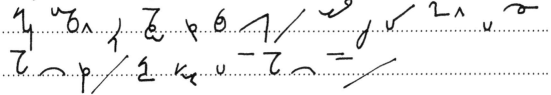

Letters Y and 1; letters G or J

–AY at the end of a word

Words ending with **-AY**, or the sound of **AY**, use indicator **A** written **downwards**.

A simple rule to remember is: if it sounds like an **A**, write an **A**

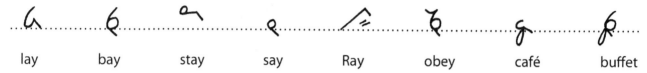

| lay | bay | stay | say | Ray | obey | café | buffet |

To help you when reading back, it is better to write full vowel **A** after **H**, **M** and **P**:

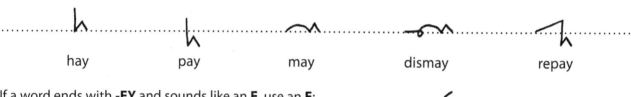

| hay | pay | may | dismay | repay |

If a word ends with **-EY** and sounds like an **E**, use an **E**:

key

1 and Y at the end of a word

Words which end with **-Y**, **-IE** or **-IGH**, but have the sound of **I**, use indicator **I**. The indicator can be written either upwards or downwards to give a clear, sharp angle.

| my | buy/by | lie | high | sigh | why | guy |

Words which end with **-Y**, but have the short sound of **I**, use indicator **I**:

| many | sorry | lady | busy | any | happy |

Y in the middle of a word

Y may be written as an **I** if it sounds like an **I**:   system

Y must be written if it has a definite sound of **Y**:   lawyer

Exercise 7.1

Read and write the following sentences.

1. ....

2. ....

3. ....

4. ....

5. ....

-LY at the end of a word

For most words which end with **-LY**, the **L** can be omitted and only indicator **I** is written. However, if the indicator does not give a clear join, write the outline in full:

| sadly | quickly | nearly | tightly | badly |

-OY in a word

If a word has **OY** in it, use Teeline letter **Y** only:

| boy | toys | Roy | royal | royalty | loyal | annoy |

Letters G or J

Write the letter **G** instead of **J** after **M** and **N** to make the words easier to write and clearer to read:

| major | enjoy | injure | injury |

Special outlines

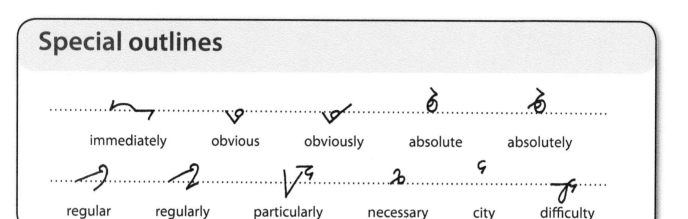

immediately   obvious   obviously   absolute   absolutely

regular   regularly   particularly   necessary   city   difficulty

Distinguishing outlines

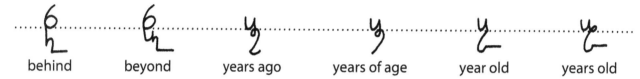

behind   beyond   years ago   years of age   year old   years old

Exercise 7.2

Read and write the following sentences.

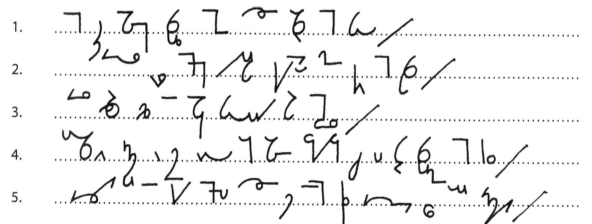

1.

2.

3.

4.

5.

Exercise 7.3 💿

Read the following passage and then prepare for dictation.

Car accident leads to injury

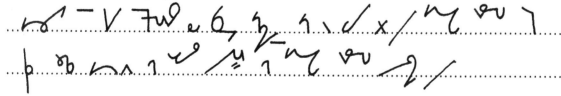

Exercise 7.4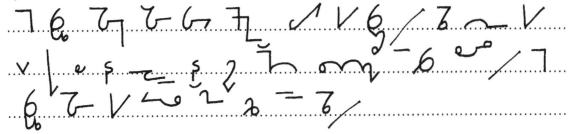

Read the following passage and then prepare for dictation.

Boys help old lady

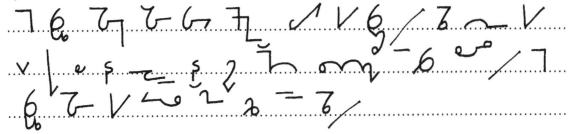

Letter L

Letter **L** has three forms to make the joining of letters easier and clearer.

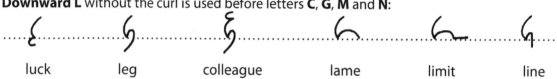

Full downward L is the more commonly used:

| leave | last | cool | low | lip | led | stool |

Downward L without the curl is used before letters **C**, **G**, **M** and **N**:

| luck | leg | colleague | lame | limit | line |

Upward L is used after **P**, **G** and **J** to prevent the outline going too far below the writing line. Upward **L** is never used at the beginning of a word:

| pull | pillow | gale | regal | jail | Jill |

Upward **L** can also be used after **H**, **M** and **N** if preferred. Note that if indicator **I** follows upward **L**, the indicator is also written upwards:

| hill | mail | nil | jolly | smelly | Nellie |

When upward **L** is followed by **T** or **D**, they are disjoined:

| pilot | pulled | halt | halted | hold | health |

Exercise 8.1

Read and write the following sentences.

1.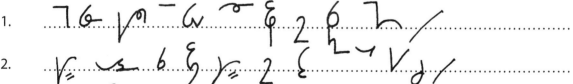

2.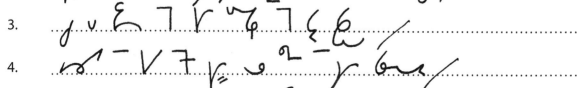

3.

4.

5.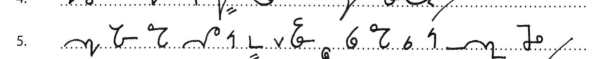

PL blend

When **P** and **L** occur together with no vowel between them at the beginning of a word, write **L** in the **P** position, through the line:

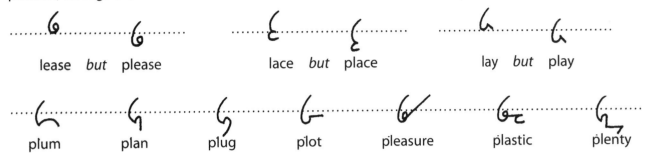

lease *but* please   lace *but* place   lay *but* play

plum   plan   plug   plot   pleasure   plastic   plenty

An initial vowel or **S** may be added:

apple   apply   supple   supply   split   splendid

In the middle or at the end of a word, **PL** is written through the preceding letter:

reply   replay   display   ample   duplicate

Exercise 8.2

Read and write the following sentences.

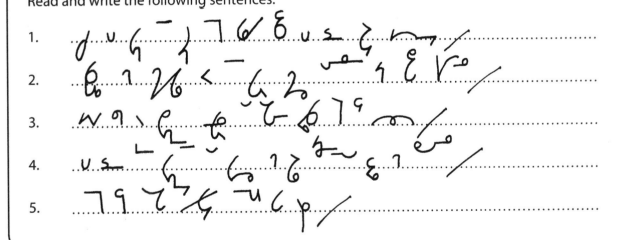

1.
2.
3.
4.
5.

Words ending –ALITY, –ELITY, –ILITY, –OLITY

Write upward **L**, disjoined, close to the previous part of the outline:

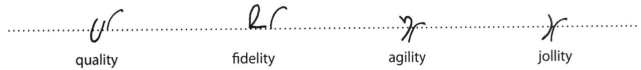

quality   fidelity   agility   jollity

Words ending -ARITY, -ERITY, -ORITY, -URITY

Write letter **R**, disjoined, close to the previous part of the outline:

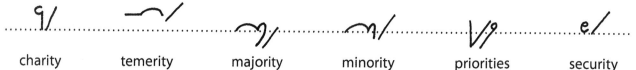

| charity | temerity | majority | minority | priorities | security |

Special outlines

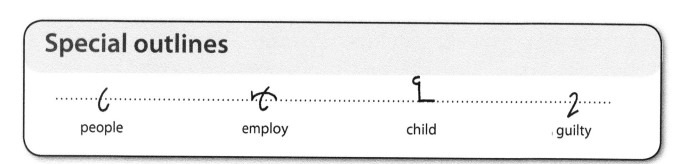

| people | employ | child | guilty |

Distinguishing outlines

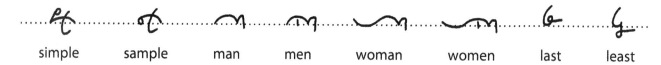

| simple | sample | man | men | woman | women | last | least |

Word groupings

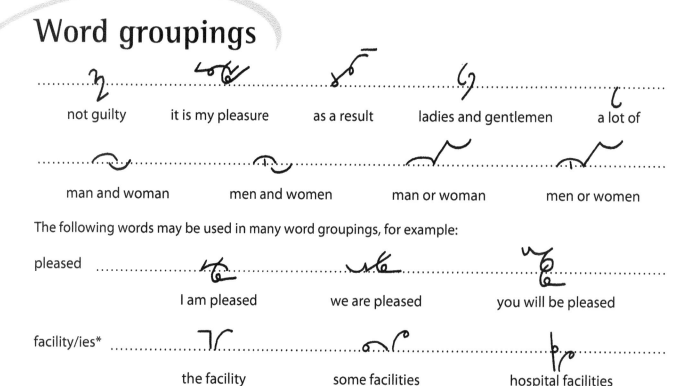

| not guilty | it is my pleasure | as a result | ladies and gentlemen | a lot of |

| man and woman | men and women | man or woman | men or women |

The following words may be used in many word groupings, for example:

pleased

| I am pleased | we are pleased | you will be pleased |

facility/ies*

| the facility | some facilities | hospital facilities |

*The word facility is written in full when standing alone

Exercise 8.3

Read and write the following sentences.

1. ....
2. ....
3. ....
4. ....
5. ....

Exercise 8.4

Read the following passage and then prepare for dictation.

How to apply to join a club

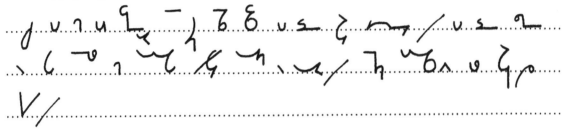

Exercise 8.5

Read the following passage and then prepare for dictation.

Hospital has good quality of care

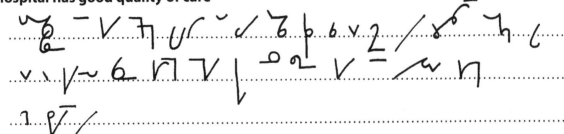

Unit 9
Use of vowels

As explained in Unit 3:

- a vowel is always written when it starts a word and when it is sounded at the end of a word
- when a word begins or ends with a double vowel, either the first or more strongly sounded vowel is written.

Letter A

Downward indicator **A** is the more commonly used:

against   adult   aboard   anger   agenda   rota   media

Upward indicator **A** is used before letters **V**, **W** and **X** to give a clear join:

avail   away   axe

The R principle

When a word begins **AR**, the **R** is omitted and the following consonant is written through full vowel **A** or written inside it:

art   artist   articles   arm   arrive   arrived

Note: do not use the **R** principle if the outline is difficult to write:

arise   arrest

Words beginning:

AUTO-

Write full vowel **A** in the **T** position:

automatic   automatically   automated

AFTER-

Write full vowel **A** on the line:

afterthought   aftercare   aftermath

AIR-, AER- or ARCH-

Write a large full vowel **A**:

air/arch   airman   aerospace   archery   architect

Exercise 9.1

Write the following words in Teeline:

again, assume, answer, media, await, avoid, arrives, army, artistic, autonomy, afterglow, airgun, aeronautic, archer, archive

Letter E

Downward indicator **E** is usually used:

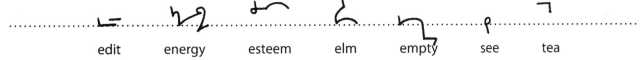

edit   energy   esteem   elm   empty   see   tea

Horizontal indicator **E** is used occasionally, usually at the end of a word, to make a clear join:

knee   pea

Full vowel **E** is used before the letters **P** and **Q** to make a clear join:

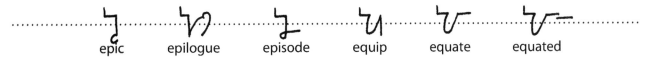

epic   epilogue   episode   equip   equate   equated

Exercise 9.2

Write the following words in Teeline:

eager, eagerly, earth, east, sea, epidemic, equity, equates

Exercise 9.3

Read and write the following sentences.

1.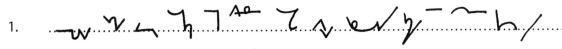
2.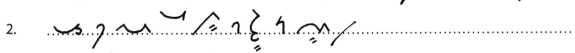
3.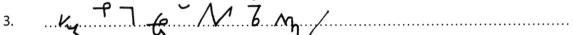
4.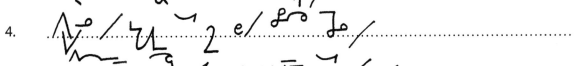
5.

Letter I

Downward indicator **I** is usually used:

ignore	idiot	indeed	impact	lie	tie

Full vowel **I** is used before **L** and **V** to give a clear join:

ill	illegal	isle	island	Ivor	ivory

Exercise 9.4

Write the following words in Teeline:

inside, immense, import, sigh, ivy, illuminate, illegitimate

Letter O

Indicator **O** is used in words beginning with **O** and ending with the sound of **O** except when the **R** principle is applied:

oak	obese	occur	olive	ogre	opposite	hello	ego

R principle

When a word begins **OR**, the **R** is omitted and the following consonant is written through full vowel **O**:

orange	ordeal	organ

O blended with N

The hook of the **N** is removed to make the outline easier to write and clearer to read:

on/one	onset	online	onslaught	lesson

O blended with M

Indicator **O** is written backwards inside letter **M**:

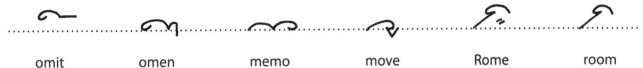

| omit | omen | memo | move | Rome | room |

Words beginning OVER-

Indicator **O** is written **over** the rest of the outline:

| overtake | overcoat | overlook | overlooked |

Exercise 9.5

Write the following words in Teeline:

oats, outlook, operate, onto, into, original, roam, Roman, ominous, overboard

---

Exercise 9.6

Read and write the following sentences.

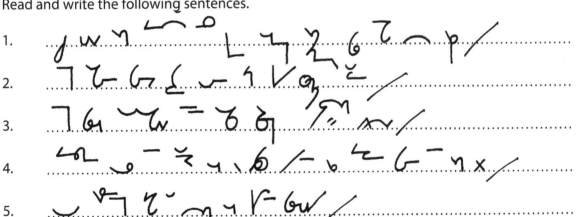

1.
2.
3.
4.
5.

Letter U

Indicator **U** is usually used:

| umpire | ugly | ultimate | ulcer | unit/unite |

Full vowel **U** is used before the letters **P**, **S** and **T** to make a clear join:

up	upon	us/use	user	utmost	utilise

Full vowel **U** is used when it is sounded at the end of a word:

clue	rescue	tissue	revue	issue	sue

R principle

When a word begins **UR**, the **R** is omitted and the following consonant is written through full vowel **U** or written inside it:

Europe	European	urge	urn

Words beginning:

UPPER-

Full vowel **U** is disjoined and written in the **T** position:

uppermost	upper-cut	upper-class

ULTRA-

Full vowel **U** is disjoined and written on the line:

ultrasound	ultraviolet

UN-

For words which have the prefix **UN-**, indicator **U** is written immediately in front of the rest of the outline and slightly above the line:

unhappy	until	unsafe	unhealthy	unrest

Exercise 9.7

Write the following words in Teeline:

united, upset, usurp, utility, sue, rue, urgent, upper-case, ultrasonic, untidy

R followed by M

Insert a vowel between **R** and **M** to make the outline easier to write and clearer to read:

ram	remain	rim	room	rum

Special outlines

or	area	ought	only	individual	opportunity

English	equivalent	member	remember	hand*

* Also used in other words, for example:

handsome	handle	handicap

Word groupings

on the other hand	no doubt	after all	over and done with

The word **over** may be used in many groupings, for example:

over the	over this	over that	over and over	over and over again

Distinguishing outlines

ease	use	easy	easier	easily	usually

Exercise 9.8

Read and write the following sentences.

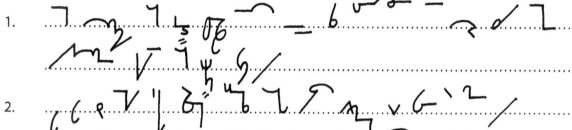

1.

2.

3.

4.

5.

Exercise 9.9

Read the following passage and then prepare for dictation.

Architect visits city

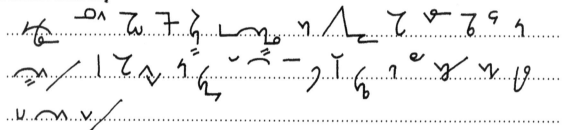

Exercise 9.10

Read the following passage and then prepare for dictation.

Visit to Europe

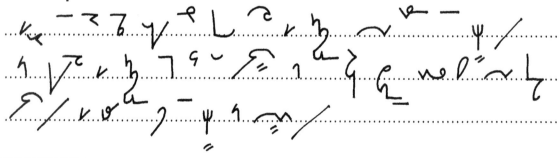

Use of vowel indicators as word endings

Vowel indicators are used to represent word endings. The indicator is written close to the previous part of the outline and is always disjoined.

-ING

The **downward** form of indicator **I** is always used:

being   willing   meeting   wing   going   sing   ring

If **-ING** is repeated, the indicator is written twice:

singing   ringing   swinging   bringing

Other letters may be added:

meetings   rings   singer   linger   lingering   winged

The word **the** may be added to **-ING**. **TH** is written to give a clear outline:

doing the   making the   having the   taking the   needing the

-ING or **-INGS** may be used to represent **thing** or **things** in word groupings:

good thing   all things   many things   most things   these things

Note: if a sentence starts with the word **things**, the outline is written in full....

-INGLE

Write letter **L**, downwards and disjoined, starting in the position of **-ING**:

single   jingles   tingled   willingly   lovingly

Exercise 10.1

Read and write the following sentences.

1.

2.

3.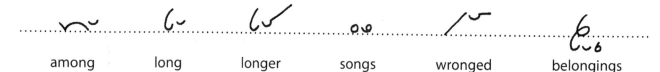

4.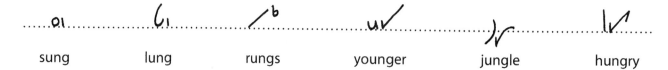

5.

–ANG

The **downward** form of indicator **A** is always used and other letters may be added:

rang	gangs	clanger	banged	pangs	tangle	hanging

–ONG

among	long	longer	songs	wronged	belongings

–UNG

sung	lung	rungs	younger	jungle	hungry

–ENG

The **downward** form of indicator **E** is always used and other letters may be added:

Feng Shui	length	lengthen	lengthy

Indicators may be used for the soft sounds of -INGE, -ANGE, -ONGE, -UNGE and -ENGE

| hinge | binge | change | range | lunge | sponge | challenge |

Special outlines

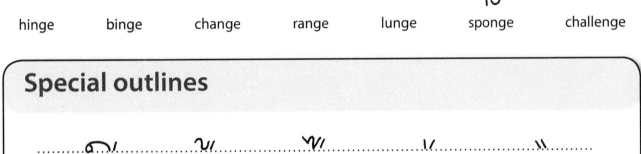

| something | nothing | anything | everything | arrange |

Word groupings

The word **else** may be used in many groupings, for example:

| something else | anything else | nothing else | everything else |

Exercise 10.2

Read and write the following sentences.

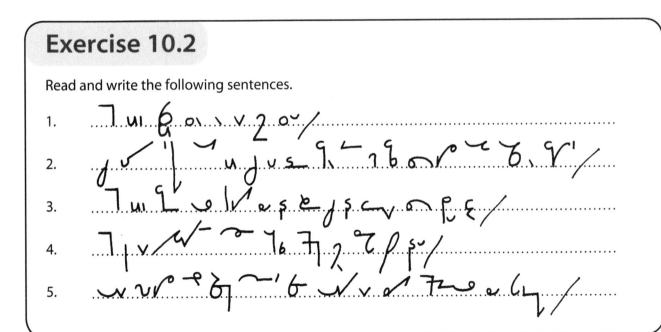

1.
2.
3.
4.
5.

Extending vowel indicators as word endings

By adding letter **C** to disjoined vowel indicators more word endings can be represented:

–ANK

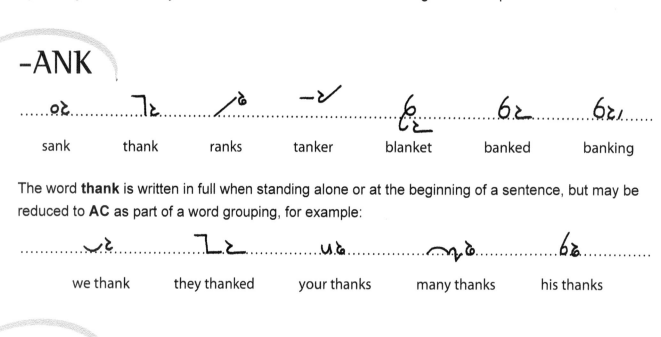

| sank | thank | ranks | tanker | blanket | banked | banking |

The word **thank** is written in full when standing alone or at the beginning of a sentence, but may be reduced to **AC** as part of a word grouping, for example:

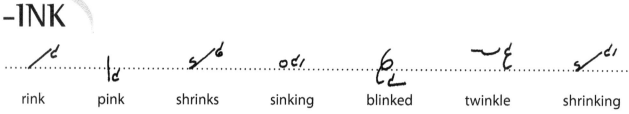

| we thank | they thanked | your thanks | many thanks | his thanks |

–INK

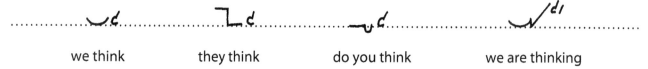

| rink | pink | shrinks | sinking | blinked | twinkle | shrinking |

The word **think** is written in full when standing alone or at the beginning of a sentence, but may be reduced to **IC** as part of a word grouping, for example:

| we think | they think | do you think | we are thinking |

–ONK

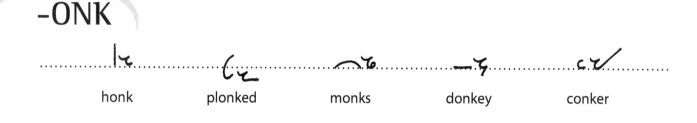

| honk | plonked | monks | donkey | conker |

–UNK

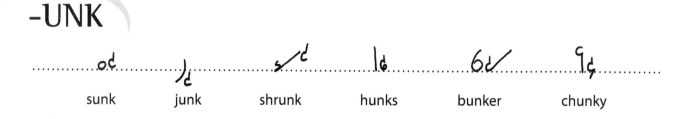

| sunk | junk | shrunk | hunks | bunker | chunky |

Special outlines

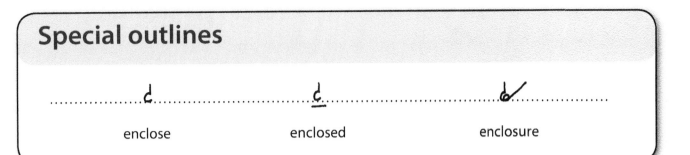

enclose · enclosed · enclosure

Word groupings

thank you · thank you for your · vote of thanks · we enclose · I think

Exercise 10.3

Read and write the following sentences.

1.
2.
3.
4.
5.

Exercise 10.4 💿

Read the following passage and then prepare for dictation.

Moving house

Exercise 10.5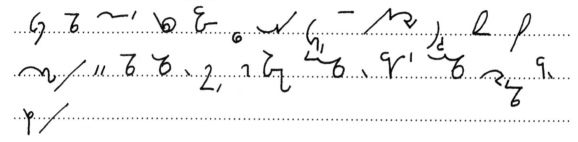

Read the following passage and then prepare for dictation.

Junk food is removed from menu

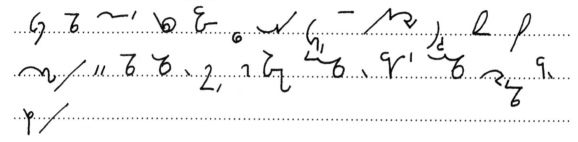

Letter F

As explained in Unit 5, letter **F** may be written upwards .... or downwards........

F may be written upwards or downwards to other letters, whichever is the clearest and easiest join.

When **F** is joined to **C**, **N**, **K** and **V**, the downward form is better, but the upward form may be used if preferred:

...... or .... or .... or .... or ......

face fun fake five

F blends

Time can be saved by blending letters together rather than joining them in their original form.

FR ....

for first farce frail freedom afraid

RF ....

rough refuse raft surf surfing

When **R** is followed by **F** and then **R** again, the blend is not used:

refer refresh referral refurbish

FL ....

fly follow film flats reflected

F blends well with several other letters

Care is needed when writing **FM** and **FW** blends so that **F** does not look like **S**:

fame family famous few wife wafer feeble fibre chief

Note: **FM** and **FW** may be written without the blend if preferred: ....

few fame

The blend is not used when **N** is followed by **F**: ....

enough knife infect

Exercise 11.1

Read and write the following sentences.

1. ⟨shorthand outline⟩
2. ⟨shorthand outline⟩
3. ⟨shorthand outline⟩
4. ⟨shorthand outline⟩
5. ⟨shorthand outline⟩

Words ending –FUL

May be written with the upward or downward **L**:

careful	beautiful	resentful	useful	hopeful	cheerfully

Words ending –FULNESS

Write **FLS** downwards, disjoined, close to the previous part of the outline:

carefulness	hopefulness	forgetfulness	usefulness	thankfulness

Words ending –LESSNESS, –LOUSNESS

Write **LS** downwards, disjoined, close to the previous part of the outline:

carelessness	helplessness	thoughtlessness	callousness

Words beginning or ending with SELF

When a word begins with **SELF-**, write the letters **SL** downwards, either joined or disjoined:

selfish	selfless	self-supporting	self-employed	self-esteem

When a word ends with **-SELF**, write the letters **SL** either upwards or downwards:

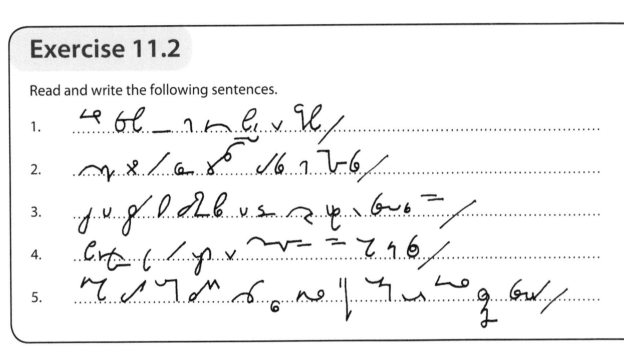

....

| myself | himself | yourself | itself | herself |

Add **S** to change words ending with **-SELF** to **-SELVES**:

....

| yourselves | themselves |

Exercise 11.2

Read and write the following sentences.

1. ....

2. ....

3. ....

4. ....

5. ....

Special outlines

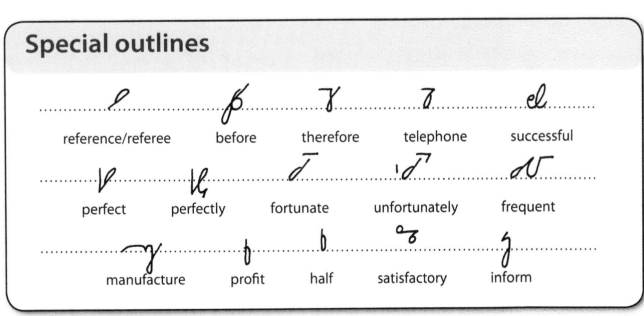

| reference/referee | before | therefore | telephone | successful |

| perfect | perfectly | fortunate | unfortunately | frequent |

| manufacture | profit | half | satisfactory | inform |

Word groupings

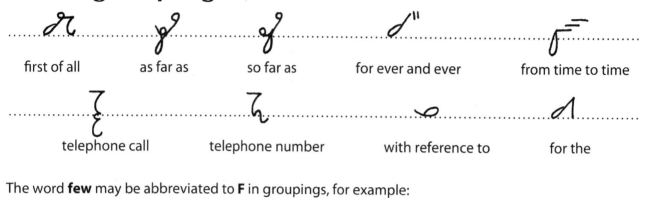

| first of all | as far as | so far as | for ever and ever | from time to time |

| telephone call | telephone number | with reference to | for the |

The word **few** may be abbreviated to **F** in groupings, for example:

last few weeks   past few years

Distinguishing outlines

firm   form   farm

Exercise 11.3

Read and write the following sentences.

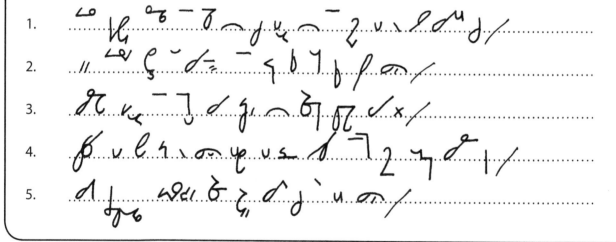

1.
2.
3.
4.
5.

Exercise 11.4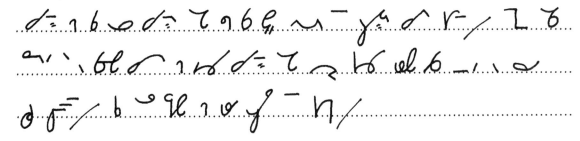

Read the following passage and then prepare for dictation.

A holiday in Africa

Exercise 11.5

Read the following passage and then prepare for dictation.

A visit to the shops

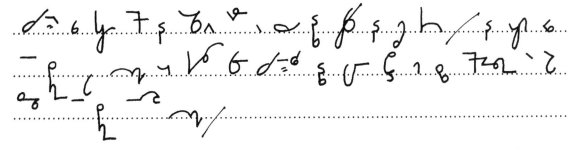

X blends, N blends and V blends

X blends

Blend **X** with other letters by writing one of the **X** strokes through the preceding or following letter.

When a word begins with **EX** it is not necessary to write vowel **E** as it can be heard in the sound of **EX**:

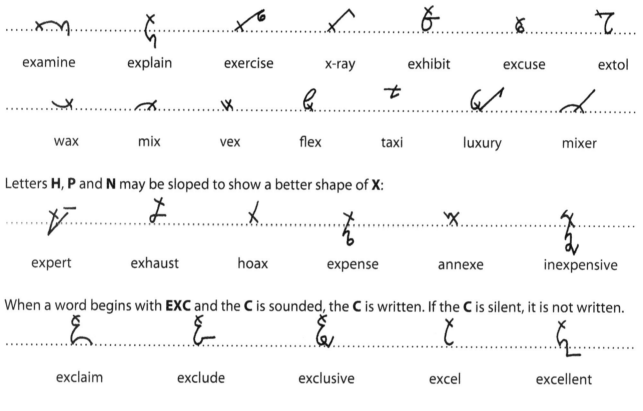

| examine | explain | exercise | x-ray | exhibit | excuse | extol |

| wax | mix | vex | flex | taxi | luxury | mixer |

Letters **H**, **P** and **N** may be sloped to show a better shape of **X**:

| expert | exhaust | hoax | expense | annexe | inexpensive |

When a word begins with **EXC** and the **C** is sounded, the **C** is written. If the **C** is silent, it is not written.

| exclaim | exclude | exclusive | excel | excellent |

Special outlines

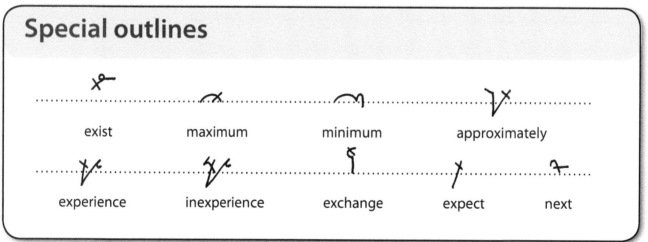

| exist | maximum | minimum | approximately |

| experience | inexperience | exchange | expect | next |

Distinguishing outlines

exceed   exact

Word groupings

for example   chief executive

Exercise 12.1

Read and write the following sentences.

1.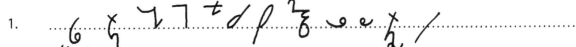
2.
3.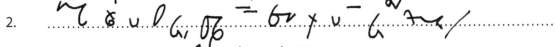
4.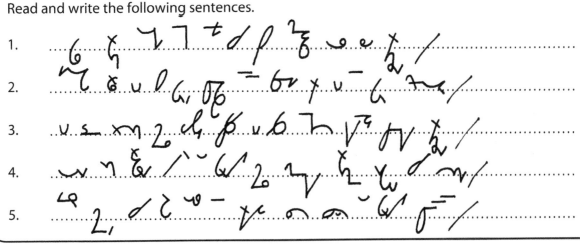
5.

N blends

NV 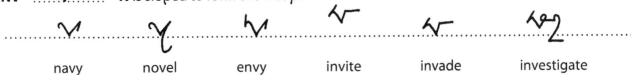 **N** is sloped to form the first part of **V**:

navy   novel   envy   invite   invade   investigate

VN 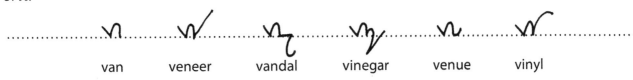 **N** follows on from **V**. Care must be taken to keep the sharp angle of **V** and the hook of **N**:

van   veneer   vandal   vinegar   venue   vinyl

RN 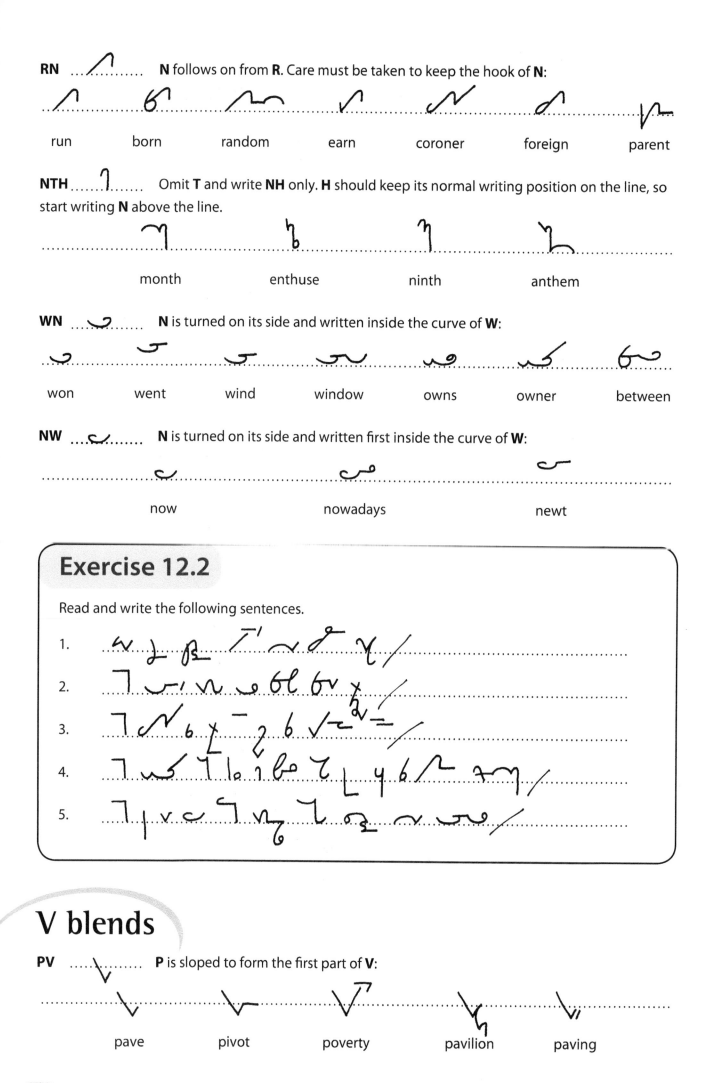   N follows on from **R**. Care must be taken to keep the hook of **N**:

run   born   random   earn   coroner   foreign   parent

NTH   Omit **T** and write **NH** only. **H** should keep its normal writing position on the line, so start writing **N** above the line.

month   enthuse   ninth   anthem

WN   N is turned on its side and written inside the curve of **W**:

won   went   wind   window   owns   owner   between

NW   N is turned on its side and written first inside the curve of **W**:

now   nowadays   newt

Exercise 12.2

Read and write the following sentences.

1.
2.
3.
4.
5.

V blends

PV   **P** is sloped to form the first part of **V**:

pave   pivot   poverty   pavilion   paving

HV .... **H** is sloped to form the first part of **V**:

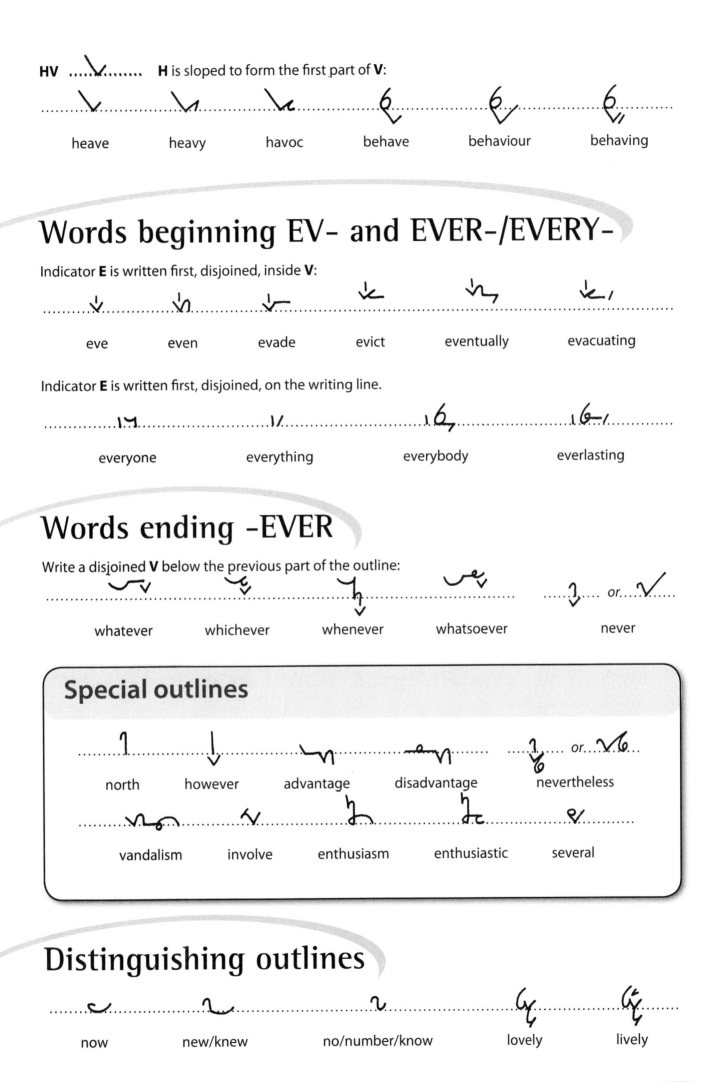

heave   heavy   havoc   behave   behaviour   behaving

Words beginning EV- and EVER-/EVERY-

Indicator **E** is written first, disjoined, inside **V**:

eve   even   evade   evict   eventually   evacuating

Indicator **E** is written first, disjoined, on the writing line.

everyone   everything   everybody   everlasting

Words ending –EVER

Write a disjoined **V** below the previous part of the outline:

whatever   whichever   whenever   whatsoever   never

Special outlines

north   however   advantage   disadvantage   nevertheless

vandalism   involve   enthusiasm   enthusiastic   several

Distinguishing outlines

now   new/knew   no/number/know   lovely   lively

Word groupings

[Teeline shorthand outlines]

they have   in the   in the north   in these days   in those days   upside down

Exercise 12.3

Read and write the following sentences.

1. *[Teeline shorthand outline]*

2. *[Teeline shorthand outline]*

3. *[Teeline shorthand outline]*

4. *[Teeline shorthand outline]*

5. *[Teeline shorthand outline]*

Exercise 12.4

Read the following passage and then prepare for dictation.

Vandalism in the town

[Teeline shorthand outline]

Exercise 12.5

Read the following passage and then prepare for dictation.

Rise in rent charges

[Teeline shorthand outline]

LR, MR and WR blends; MB and PB blends

Letters **L**, **M** and **W** are lengthened to add **R**. They are written about double the usual length and may or may not have a vowel in between.

LR blend

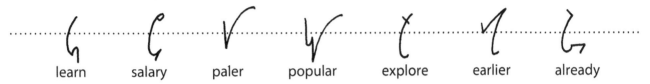

learn salary paler popular explore earlier already

MR blend

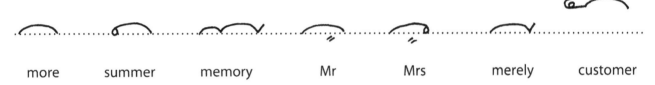

more summer memory Mr Mrs merely customer

WR blend

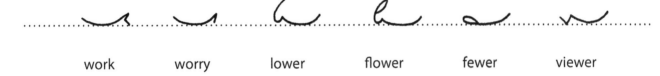

work worry lower flower fewer viewer

Special outlines

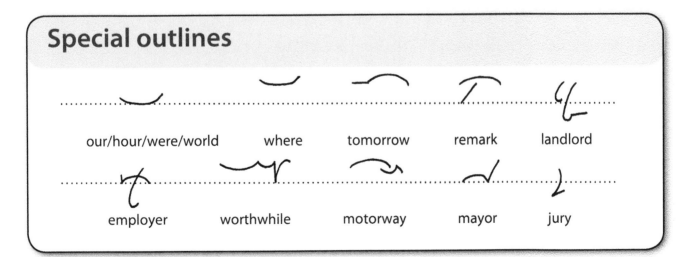

our/hour/were/world where tomorrow remark landlord

employer worthwhile motorway mayor jury

Distinguishing outlines

smaller

similar

Word groupings

more and more

more or less

smaller and smaller

larger and larger

this morning

sum of money

sums of money

all parts of the world

in our

Mr and Mrs

Write downward indicator **A** over the rest of the outline to represent the words **all over the**:

all over the world

all over the town

all over the place

all over the city

Exercise 13.1

Read and write the following sentences.

1.

2.

3.

4.

5.

MB blend

Write circle **B** after **M**, taking care to write it larger than circle **S**:

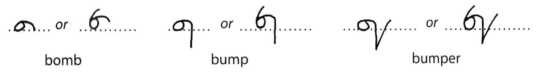

| mob | mobs | mobile | automobile | symbol |

Circle **B** may be used before **M**, but full letter **B** may be used if preferred:

| bomb | bump | bumper |

PB blend

Write circle **B** on the side of **P**:

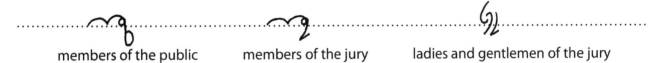

| public* | republic | publish | puberty | publicity |

*special outline

Special outlines

public

Word groupings

| members of the public | members of the jury | ladies and gentlemen of the jury |

The word **opinion** may be represented by letter **P** sloping in the direction of downward indicator **I** and written through the previous part of the outline:

| our opinion | in our opinion | your opinion | my opinion |

It is written in full when standing alone or at the start of a sentence:

Exercise 13.2 🎧

Read the following passage and then prepare for dictation.

Accidents on the motorway

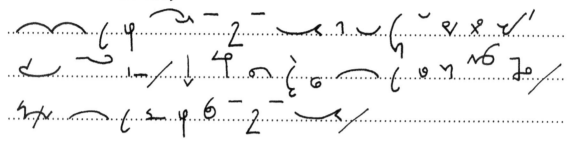

Exercise 13.3 🎧

Read the following passage and then prepare for dictation.

Meeting of landlords in the town

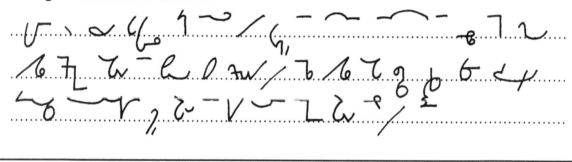

Unit 14
The R principle – BR, CR, GR and PR

The **R** principle has already been used for full vowels **A**, **O** and **U**, for example:

art   ordeal   urge

The same principle is applied to letters **B**, **C**, **G** and **P**. However, when a vowel occurs between **B** and **R**, **C** and **R**, **G** and **R** and **P** and **R**, the outline is written in full:

BR

break   bright   brown   bribe   abbreviate   brag

broad *but* board   bridge *but* barge   bran *but* barn

CR

crime   creep   credit   crown   cracked   craft

crude *but* card   crave *but* carve   crab *but* curb

GR

grim   grown   grave   grip   aggravate   aggressive

grade *but* guard   grill *but* girl   regret *but* regard

PR

product   protect   promote   produce   promise   prowl

When **PR** is followed by a vertical letter, or it is difficult to intersect through **P**, write the rest of the outline close to the **P**:

propose   proper   apprehend   present   provide   private

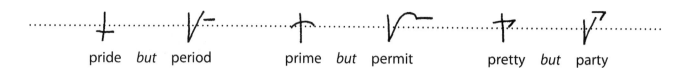

pride *but* period   prime *but* permit   pretty *but* party

If an outline is difficult to write using the **R** principle, simply write it in full:

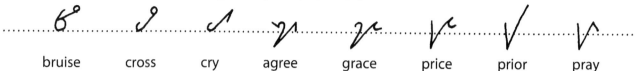

bruise   cross   cry   agree   grace   price   prior   pray

Exercise 14.1

Read and write the following sentences.

1.
2.
3.
4.
5.

Special outlines

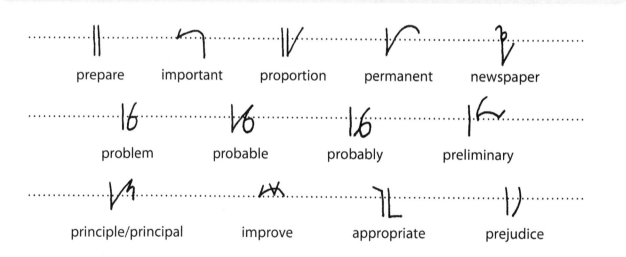

prepare   important   proportion   permanent   newspaper

problem   probable   probably   preliminary

principle/principal   improve   appropriate   prejudice

Distinguishing outlines

press   papers

Word groupings

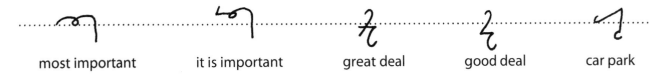

most important   it is important   great deal   good deal   car park

Exercise 14.2

Read and write the following sentences.

1.
2.
3.
4.
5.

Exercise 14.3 💿

Read the following passage and then prepare for dictation.

The level of crime is growing

Exercise 14.4 🔘

Read the following passage and then prepare for dictation.

Opportunity to improve career prospects

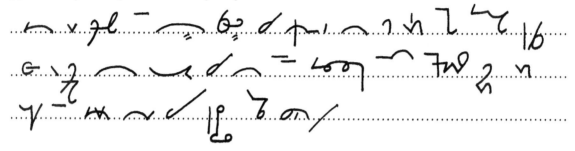

Words ending –SHUN, –SHL, –SHIP and –SHUS

Words ending –SHUN

Letter **N** written in the **T** position, disjoined and close to the previous part of the outline, represents the sound of **-SHUN**, no matter how it is spelt:

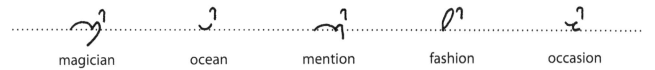

| magician | ocean | mention | fashion | occasion |

Other letters may be added:

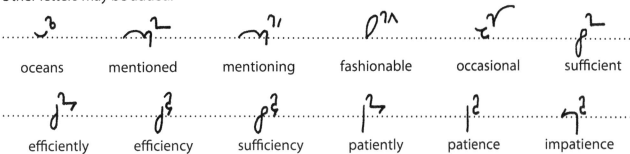

| oceans | mentioned | mentioning | fashionable | occasional | sufficient |

| efficiently | efficiency | sufficiency | patiently | patience | impatience |

Exercise 15.1

Read and write the following sentences.

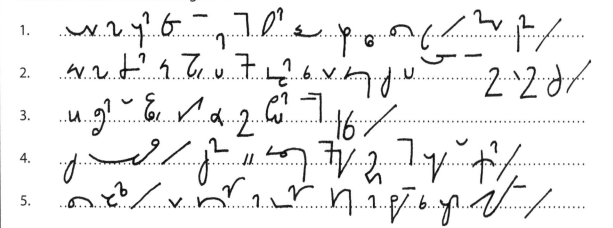

1.
2.
3.
4.
5.

Words ending –SHL

SH is written disjoined and close to the previous part of the outline to represent the sound of **-SHL**, no matter how it is spelt:

special   official   racial   marshal   essential   initial

Other letters may be added:

especially   officialdom   speciality   marshals   essentially

---

Exercise 15.2

Read and write the following sentences.

1. ....

2. ....

3. ....

Words ending –SHIP

SH is joined to the outline:

hardship   friendship   relationships   battleships

Exercise 15.3

Read and write the following sentences.

1. ....

2. ....

3. ....

Words ending -SHUS

SHS is joined to the previous part of the outline and represents the sound of **-SHUS**, no matter how it is spelt:

delicious   vicious   gracious   precious   cautious   anxious

Exercise 15.4

Read and write the following sentences.

1.

2.

3.

Special outlines

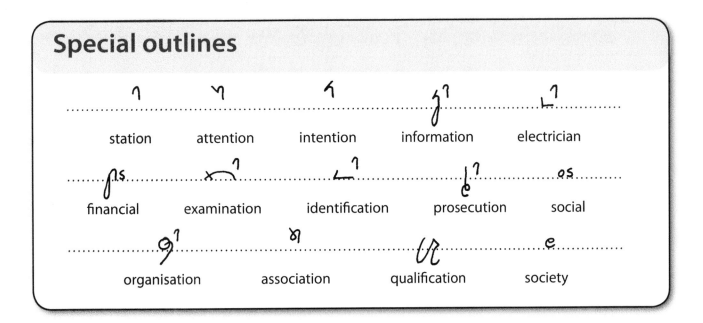

station   attention   intention   information   electrician

financial   examination   identification   prosecution   social

organisation   association   qualification   society

Distinguishing outlines

specialist   specialised

Exercise 15.5 🔘

Read the following passage and then prepare for dictation.

Theft at jeweller's shop

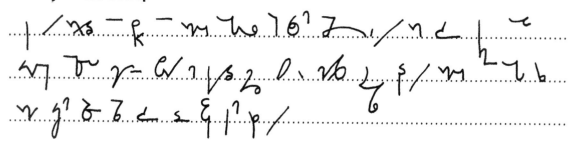

Exercise 15.6 🔘

Read the following passage and then prepare for dictation.

Good qualifications are important

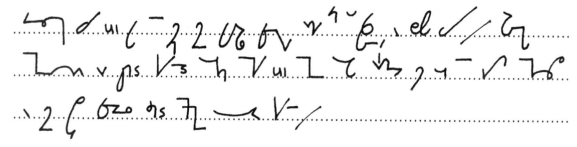

Unit 16
T and D blends

TR blend

Letters **T** and **R** may be blended together by lengthening the **T**. It does not matter if the letters **TR** occur together or if there is a vowel in the middle. The blend may be used anywhere in the outline:

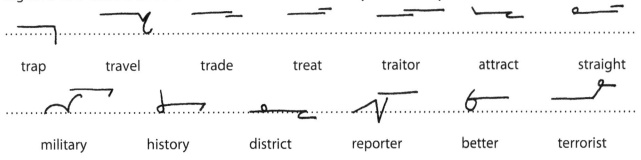

trap	travel	trade	treat	traitor	attract	straight

military	history	district	reporter	better	terrorist

DR blend

Similarly, letters **D** and **R** may be blended together by lengthening the **D**. It does not matter if the letters **DR** occur together or if there is a vowel in the middle. The blend may be used anywhere in the outline:

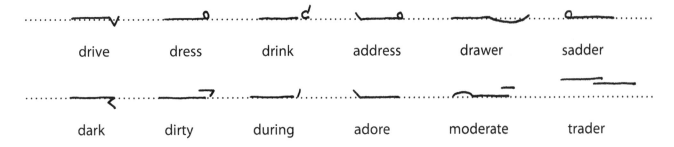

drive	dress	drink	address	drawer	sadder

dark	dirty	during	adore	moderate	trader

Exercise 16.1

Read and write the following sentences.

1.
2.
3.
4.
5.

TN and DN blends

Letters **T** and **D** can both be blended with **N** by smoothing out the hook of **N**. Care must be taken to retain the curve of **N** so that it does not look like indicator **E**:

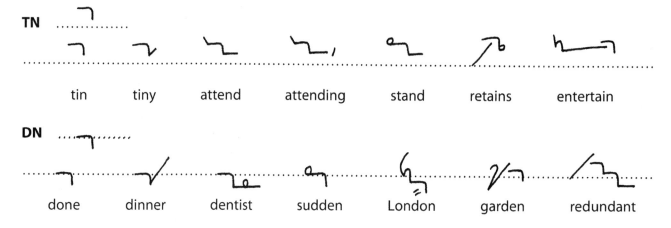

tin	tiny	attend	attending	stand	retains	entertain

done	dinner	dentist	sudden	London	garden	redundant

TRN and DRN blends

Blends **TR** and **DR** can be extended to add the blend of **N**:

train	return	strain	restaurant	drain	drainage	modern

THR blend

The **TR** blend may also be used to represent **THR** when it occurs in the middle or at the end of a word:

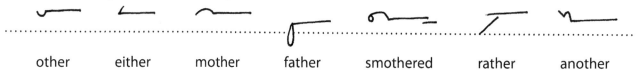

other	either	mother	father	smothered	rather	another

The **THR** blend is not used at the beginning of a word:

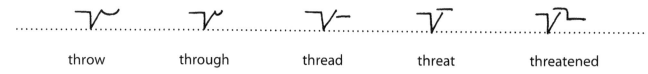

throw	through	thread	threat	threatened

CTR blend

The **CT** blend (Unit 5) can be extended to add **R**:

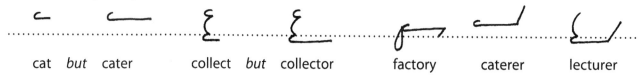

cat	*but* cater	collect	*but* collector	factory	caterer	lecturer

Exercise 16.2

Read and write the following sentences.

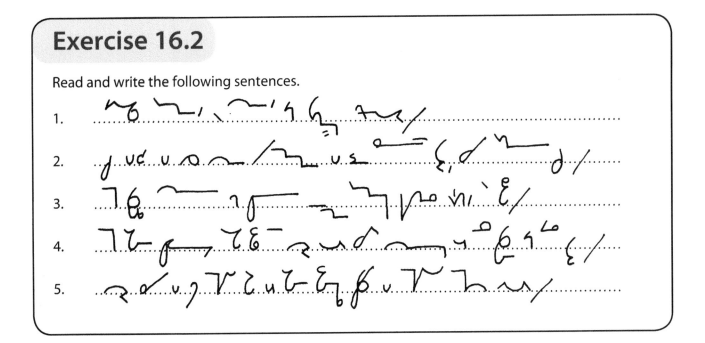

1.
2.
3.
4.
5.

Words beginning TRANS-

Write the letters **TRS** and omit **N**:

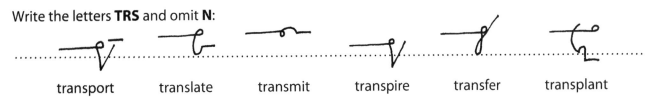

transport   translate   transmit   transpire   transfer   transplant

Words beginning UNDER-

Write the letters **UDR** (use full vowel **U**) and omit **N**:

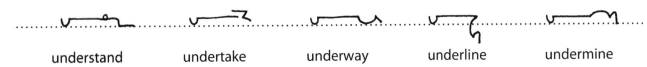

understand   undertake   underway   underline   undermine

Words ending –NESS

When a word ends with a strongly sounded **-NESS**, write full letter **N** followed by **S**:

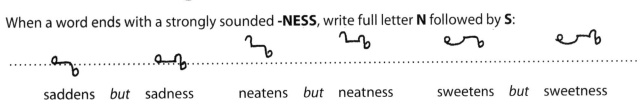

saddens *but* sadness   neatens *but* neatness   sweetens *but* sweetness

Special outlines

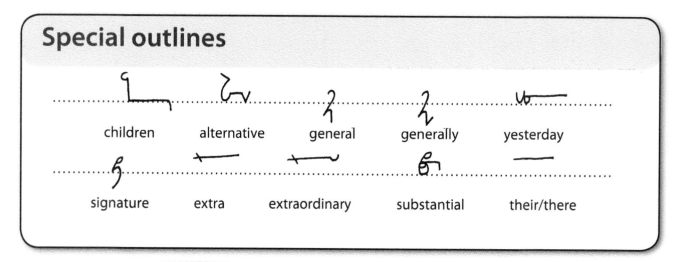

children   alternative   general   generally   yesterday

signature   extra   extraordinary   substantial   their/there

Distinguishing outlines

feature   future   farther   further

Word groupings

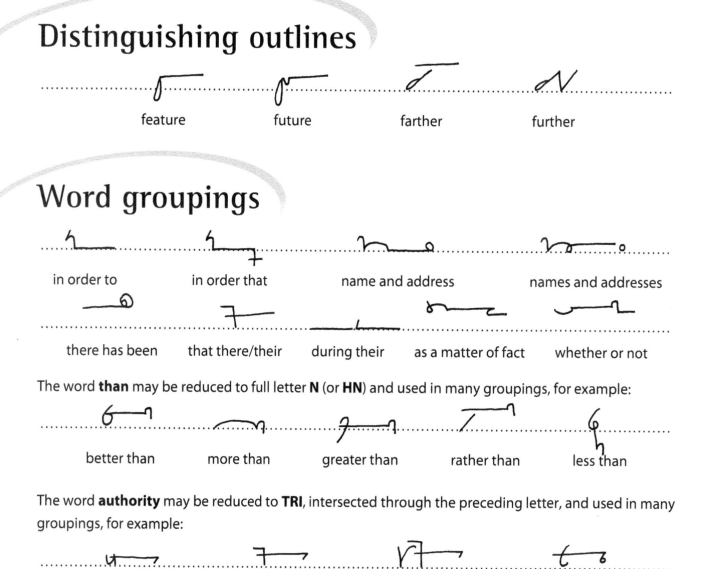

in order to   in order that   name and address   names and addresses

there has been   that there/their   during their   as a matter of fact   whether or not

The word **than** may be reduced to full letter **N** (or **HN**) and used in many groupings, for example:

better than   more than   greater than   rather than   less than

The word **authority** may be reduced to **TRI**, intersected through the preceding letter, and used in many groupings, for example:

your authority   the authority   health authority   local authorities

Note: if a sentence starts with **authority**, the outline is written in full ....

Exercise 16.3

Read and write the following sentences.

1. ....

2. ....

3. ....

4. ....

5. ....

Exercise 16.4

Read the following passage and then prepare for dictation.

Local authority improves leisure facilities

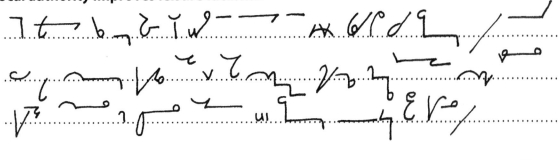

Exercise 16.5

Read the following passage and then prepare for dictation.

Downturn in sales

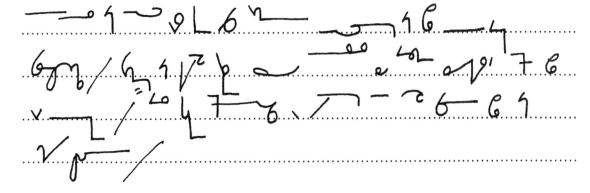

Letter C

CM blend

CM ....⌒....... The **CM** blend is formed by writing letter **C** the width of letter **M**. It represents **C** vowel **M** and is used for either the hard or soft sound of **C**:

camp	campaign	chemist	complete	welcome	cemetery

scheme	scamp	accommodate	accommodation	accompanying

Insert a vowel if the outline is difficult to write:

common	uncommon	camera	cement/comment

Words beginning ENCOM-, INCOM-

Omit **N** and join the initial vowel to **CM** to avoid an awkward outline:

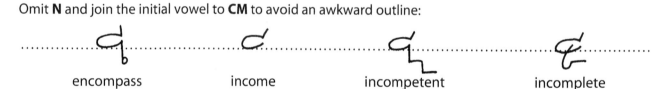

encompass	income	incompetent	incomplete

Words beginning RECOM-

Write **RC** only, disjoined:

recompense	recommend*	recommendation

*special outline

Read and write the following sentences.

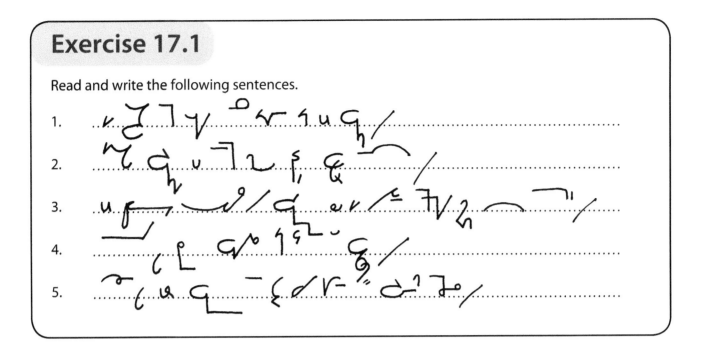

1.
2.
3.
4.
5.

Words ending –NCE

Write a disjoined letter **C** close to the previous part of the outline:

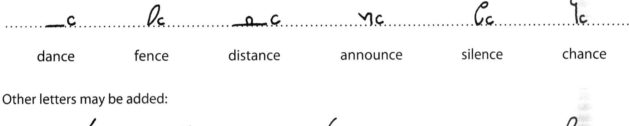

| dance | fence | distance | announce | silence | chance |

Other letters may be added:

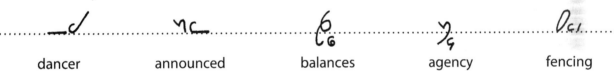

| dancer | announced | balances | agency | fencing |

Words ending –NCH

Write a disjoined **CH** on the writing line close to the previous part of the outline:

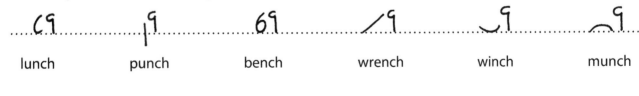

| lunch | punch | bench | wrench | winch | munch |

Other letters may be added:

| luncheon | punched | benches | munching |

Special outlines

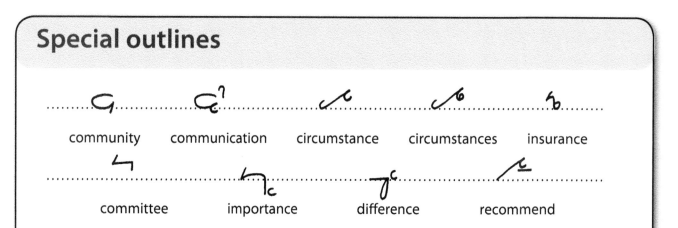

community	communication	circumstance	circumstances	insurance

committee	importance	difference	recommend

Distinguishing outlines

come	came	become	became

Word groupings

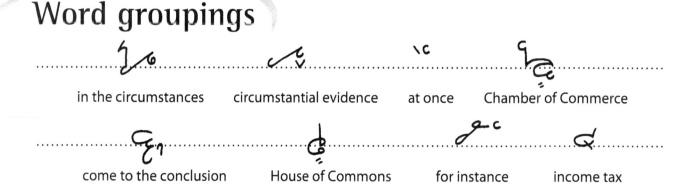

in the circumstances	circumstantial evidence	at once	Chamber of Commerce

come to the conclusion	House of Commons	for instance	income tax

Exercise 17.2

Read and write the following sentences.

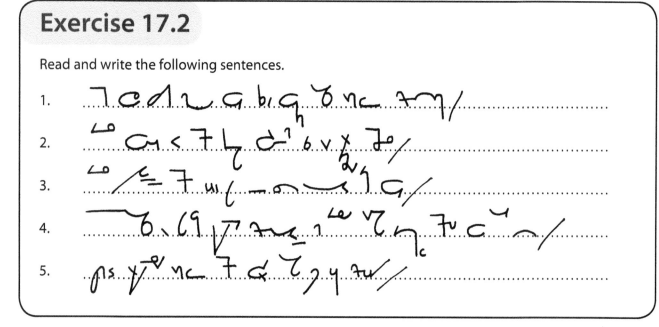

1.
2.
3.
4.
5.

CN blend

CN ......⌐........ The **CN** blend is formed by writing letter **N** in the direction of letter **C**. It represents **C** vowel **N** and is used for either the hard or soft sound of **C**:

can	candle	scandal	economy	control/central	applicant

cinema	censor	census	concentrate	cinder

taken/token	mistaken

When **CN** is preceded by a vowel and letter **N**, omit **N**:

encounter	inconsiderate	incentive	inconclusive

CNV blend

CNV .....⌄........ Slope **CN** to form the first part of letter **V**:

canvas	converse	conversation	converge	convince	convey

convex	convert	convene	convent	convention	conventional

Exercise 17.3

Read and write the following sentences.

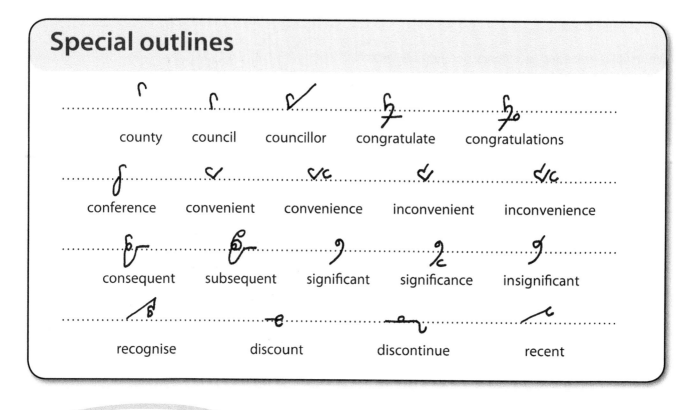

Special outlines

county	council	councillor	congratulate	congratulations

conference	convenient	convenience	inconvenient	inconvenience

consequent	subsequent	significant	significance	insignificant

recognise	discount	discontinue	recent

Word groupings

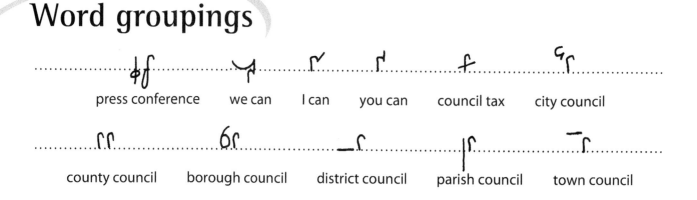

press conference	we can	I can	you can	council tax	city council

county council	borough council	district council	parish council	town council

The following words can be used in many word groupings, for example:

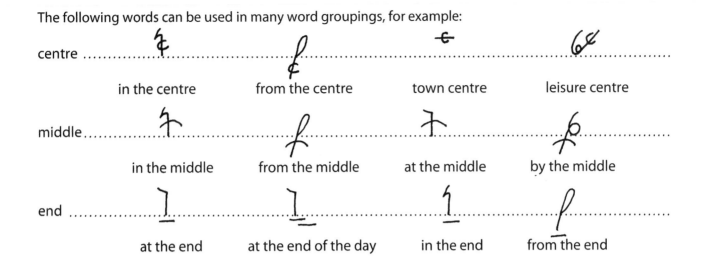

centre

in the centre   from the centre   town centre   leisure centre

middle

in the middle   from the middle   at the middle   by the middle

end

at the end   at the end of the day   in the end   from the end

Exercise 17.4

Read and write the following sentences.

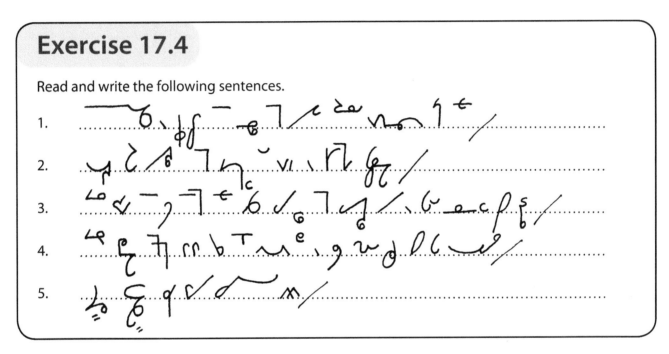

1.

2.

3.

4.

5.

Exercise 17.5 💿

Read the following passage and then prepare for dictation.

Park Road flats to be condemned

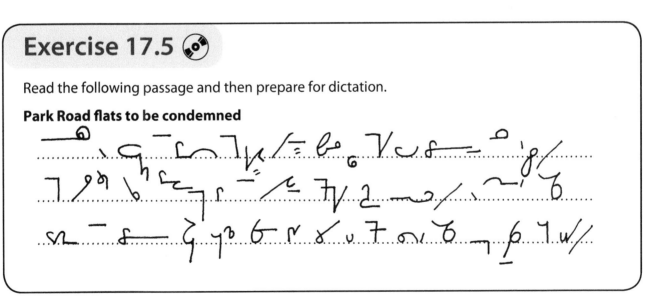

Exercise 17.6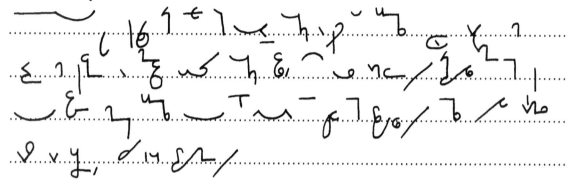

Read the following passage and then prepare for dictation.

Youths cause problems in the town centre

NCTJ Teeline Gold Standard for Journalists

Numbers, currencies, measurements, abbreviations and colloquialisms

Numbers

Numbers between **1** and **99** may be written as ordinary figures, but numbers **1, 6** and **7** should be circled to avoid confusion with Teeline outlines (**1** could be mistaken for **he** or **a**, **6** could be mistaken for **be/been** and **7** could be mistaken for **the**).

①	⑥	⑦	8	9	10	
1	6	7	8	9	10	*etc.*

Numbers higher than **99** should be written as follows:

Hundred – **DR** blend under the figure:

	100	a hundred	500

Thousand – letter **T** above the figure:

3000

Million – letter **M** under the figure:

4,000,000

Hundred thousand – **DR** blend and **T** above it:

500,000

Hundred million – **DR** blend and **M** under the figure:

800,000,000

Billion – letter **B** next to the figure
(circle the figure to avoid the danger of
misreading **B** as number 6, i.e. 56)

5,000,000,000

Word groupings may be incorporated :

many hundreds of   there were thousands of

If the words cannot be written with a figure or as part of a word grouping, then the full outline should be written:

hundred   thousand   million   billion

Fractions – written as normal but without the dividing line:

2/3

Per cent – write **PR** next to the figure:

25%

Currencies

Pounds Sterling – write a dot after the figure:

£3   £300

Euro – Full vowel **U** with indicator **O** written through it:

€25

Dollar – **DS** under the figure:

$5 $500

Dates – for years beginning 2000 write the last 2 digits:

2003

– for years prior to 2000 write the date in full:

1967   1826

Century – write a large **C** around the figure or word:

21st century   last century

Measurements

Gram – letter **G** next to the figure:

20 grams

Kilogram – **KG** next to the figure:

5 kilograms

Metre – **MR** blend in the **T** position: .... 40 [shorthand outline]

40 metres

Centimetre – **CN** and **MR** blends in the **T** position: .... 8 [shorthand outline]

8 centimetres

Kilometre – **K** and **MR** blend in the **T** position: .... 3̄ [shorthand outline]

3,000 kilometres

Millimetre – **M** and **MR** blend in the **T** position: .... 9 [shorthand outline]

9 millimetres

Litre – **LR** blend written **downwards**: .... 12 [shorthand outline]

12 litres

Millilitre – **M** and **LR** blend written **upwards**: .... 4 [shorthand outline]

4 millilitres

Abbreviations

Words and phrases may be abbreviated in Teeline, but they must be transcribed in full if they are dictated in full. To indicate that a word or phrase should be transcribed in full, write a squiggly line under the outline:

[shorthand outlines] MP   *but*   Member of Parliament

[shorthand outlines] NHS   *but*   National Health Service

[shorthand outlines] UK   *but*   United Kingdom

[shorthand outlines] CCTV   *but*   closed-circuit television

Days of the week:

Sunday ....[shorthand].... Monday .....[shorthand]..... Tuesday ....[shorthand]....

Wednesday ....[shorthand].... Thursday ....[shorthand].... Friday ....[shorthand]....

Saturday ....[shorthand]....

Months of the year:

January ....

February ....

March ....

April............................

May ....

June ....

July ....

August ....

September............................

October ....

November ....

December ....

Colloquialisms

If colloquial speech is used, an apostrophe should be written as part of the outline:

I'm *but* I am   it's *but* it is   I've *but* I have

Word groupings

Use a dot to represent the words **point** and **spot**:

come straight to the point   point of view   on the spot

Exercise 18.1

Read and write the following sentences.

1.

2.

3.

4.

5.

Exercise 18.2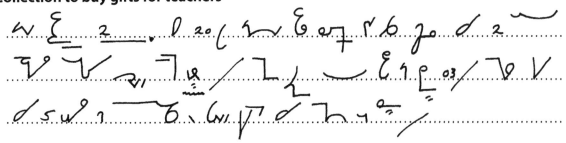

Read the following passage and then prepare for dictation.

Collection to buy gifts for teachers

More word endings

Full vowels as word endings

Full vowel A, disjoined, written close to the previous part of the outline, represents **-ABLE** or **-ABILITY**:

capable/capability   desirable/desirability   available/availability

Other letters may be added to extend the word ending:

tables   stables   labelling   disabled   favourably   reasonably

Full vowel I, disjoined, written close to the previous part of the outline, represents **-IBLE** or **-IBILITY**:

visible/visibility   sensible/sensibility   compatible/compatibility

Indicator **I** may be added to full vowel **I** to represent **-IBLY**:

possibly   legibly   terribly

Full vowel E, disjoined, written close to the previous part of the outline, represents **-EB(B)LE** or **-EBEL**. Other letters may be added to extend the word ending:

rebel   pebbles   pebbly   treble   trebling

Full vowel O, disjoined, written close to the previous part of the outline, represents **-OB(B)LE, -OUBLE** or **-OBILITY**. Other letters may be added to extend the word ending:

noble/nobility   hobble   troubled   doubles   wobbly

Full vowel U, disjoined, written close to the previous part of the outline, represents **-UB(B)LE** or **-UBILITY**. Other letters may be added to extend the word ending:

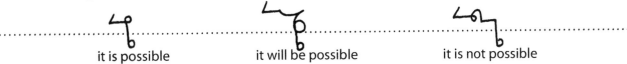

| soluble/solubility | stubble | bubbles | bubbly | rubble |

Word groupings

| it is possible | it will be possible | it is not possible |

Exercise 19.1

Read and write the following sentences.

1.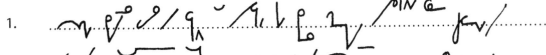

2.

3.

4.

5.

-WOOD, -WORD, -WARD, -WIDE

Write a small letter **W** (about half the normal size) below the previous part of the outline. Other letters may be added to extend the word ending:

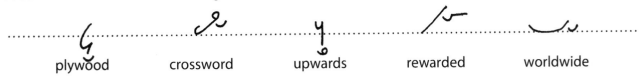

| plywood | crossword | upwards | rewarded | worldwide |

Small **W** can be used in word groupings:

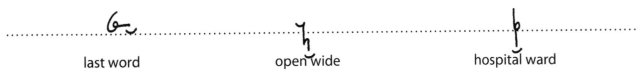

| last word | open wide | hospital ward |

The word **forward** may be reduced to a small **W** in word groupings:

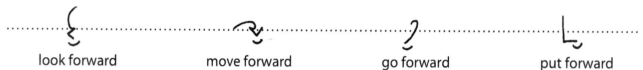

look forward   move forward   go forward   put forward

–MENT

Write a small letter **M**, disjoined, in the **T** position and close to the previous part of the outline. Other letters may be added to extend the word ending:

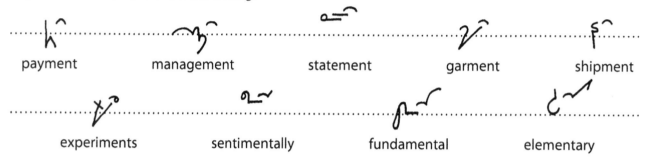

payment   management   statement   garment   shipment

experiments   sentimentally   fundamental   elementary

Exercise 19.2

Read and write the following sentences.

1.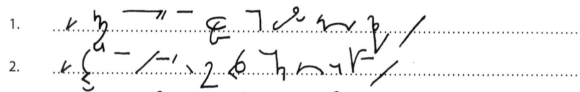

2.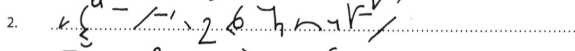

3.

4.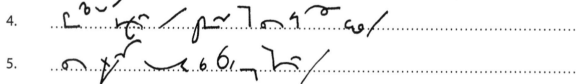

5.

–AVITY, –EVITY

Write letter **V**, disjoined, in the **T** position and close to the previous part of the outline:

cavity   gravity   brevity   longevity

-TIVITY

Write **TV**, disjoined, in the **T** position close to the previous part of the outline:

| activity | productivity | relativity | sensitivity |

-OVER

Write **VR**, below the previous part of the outline:

| takeover | hangover | changeover | flyover | all over |

Exercise 19.3

Read and write the following sentences.

1.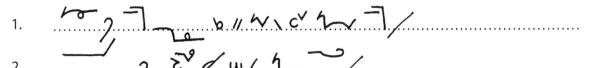
2.
3.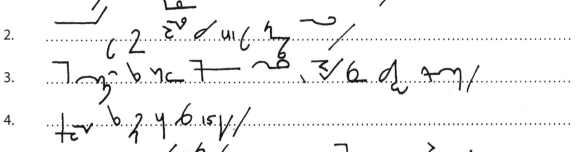
4.
5.

-JECT

Write letter **J**, joined or disjoined, close to the previous part of the outline. Other letters may be added to extend the word ending:

| inject | subject | subjects | rejected | objective | objection |

-GRAM

Write **GM**, joined to the previous part of the outline. Other letters may be added to extend the word ending:

diagram	monogram	mammogram	anagrams	programmer

-GRAPH

Write **GF** blended together, joined to the previous part of the outline. Other letters may be added to extend the word ending:

autograph	telegraph	paragraphs	photographer	geography

-OLOGY, -ALOGY

Write indicator **O**, disjoined and in the **T** position:

biology	sociology	psychology	meteorology	genealogy

-OLOGICAL, -ALOGICAL

Add letter **L** to indicator **O**:

biological	psychological	genealogical

-OLOGIST

Add **ST** to indicator **O**:

biologist	zoologist	sociologist

Special outlines

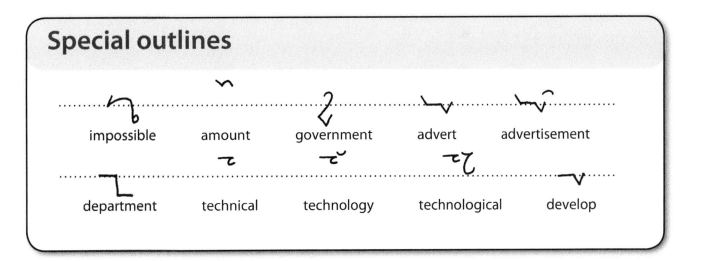

| impossible | amount | government | advert | advertisement |

| department | technical | technology | technological | develop |

Distinguishing outlines

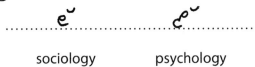

sociology   psychology

Word groupings

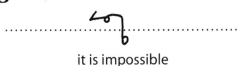

it is impossible

Exercise 19.4

Read and write the following sentences.

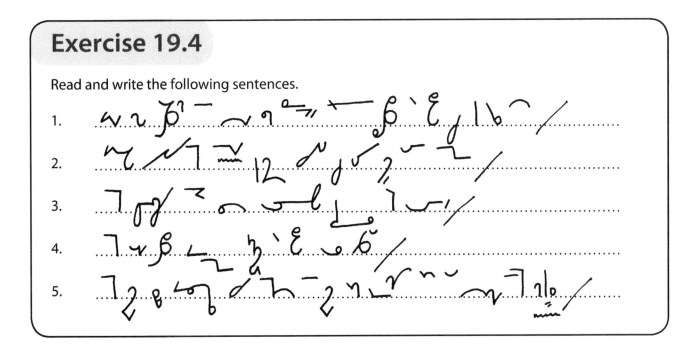

1.
2.
3.
4.
5.

Exercise 19.5

Read the following passage and then prepare for dictation.

Eating sensibly

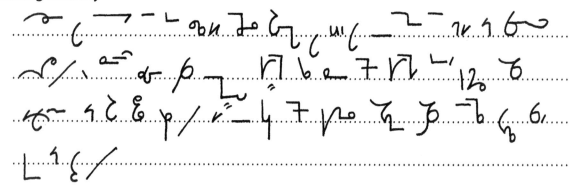

Exercise 19.6

Read the following passage and then prepare for dictation.

Advertisement in *The Telegraph*

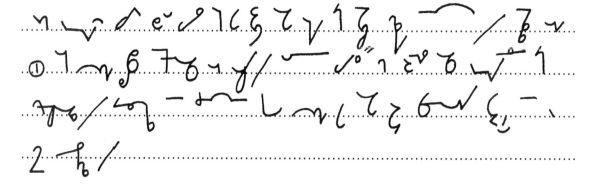

More word beginnings

INC-, ENC-

Omit letter **N**:

encourage   encore   encroach   include   increase   incur

INS-, INT-

Omit letter **N**:

insure   instance   inspire   intimidate   interest   intruder

SUPER-

Write letter **S** with indicator **U**, disjoined, above the rest of the outline:

supervise   supervisor   supersede   superhuman   supernatural

ABOVE-

Write letter **V above** the rest of the outline:

above-named   above-average   above-mentioned   over and above

Read and write the following sentences.

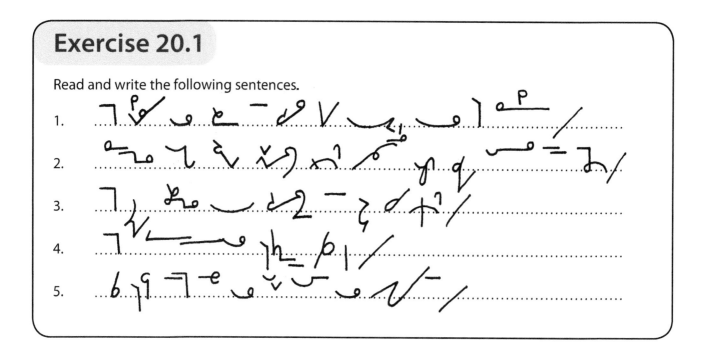

1.
2.
3.
4.
5.

MULTI-

Write letter **M** above the rest of the outline:

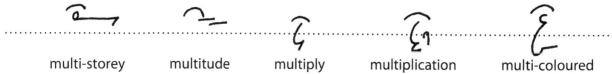

| multi-storey | multitude | multiply | multiplication | multi-coloured |

NATION-, NON-

Write a large loop to indicate two letter **N**s:

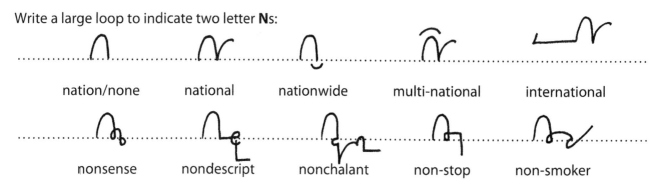

| nation/none | national | nationwide | multi-national | international |
| nonsense | nondescript | nonchalant | non-stop | non-smoker |

SEMI-

Write letter **S**, disjoined, immediately in front of the rest of the outline:

| semi-final | semi-circle | semi-detached | semi-conscious |

ANTI-, ANTE-, ANTA-

Write **AN**, disjoined and in the **T** position, close to the rest of the outline:

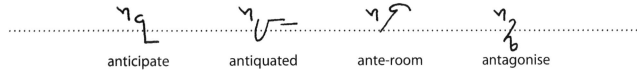

anticipate   antiquated   ante-room   antagonise

Exercise 20.2

Read and write the following sentences.

1. ....
2. ....
3. ....
4. ....
5. ....

ELECTRI-, ELECTRO-

Write full vowel **E**, disjoined, immediately in front of the rest of the outline:

electrify   electroplate   electrocute   electrode

MAGNA-, MAGNE-, MAGNI-, MAGNO-

Write **MG**, disjoined, immediately in front of the rest of the outline:

magnanimous   magnetic   magnificent   magnolia

MICRO-

Write **MC**, disjoined, immediately in front of the rest of the outline:

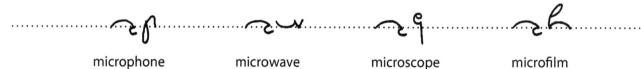

| microphone | microwave | microscope | microfilm |

Special outlines

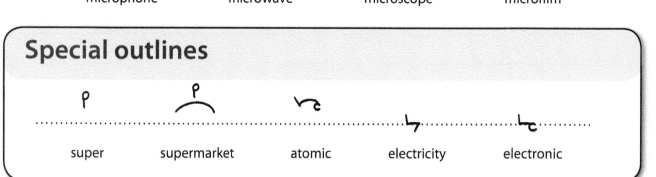

| super | supermarket | atomic | electricity | electronic |

Word groupings

multi-storey car park   at home and abroad   anti-social behaviour   anti-social behaviour order

Exercise 20.3

Read and write the following sentences.

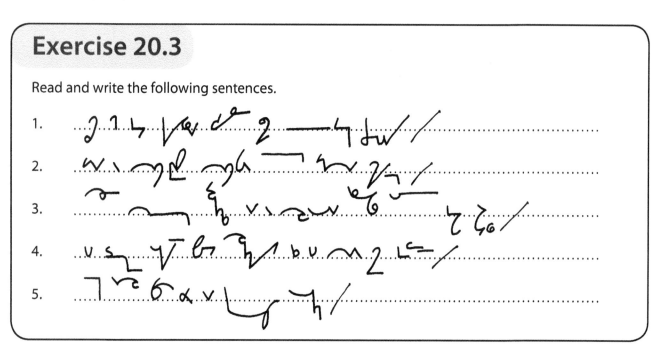

1.
2.
3.
4.
5.

Exercise 20.4

Read the following passage and then prepare for dictation.

Using the Internet

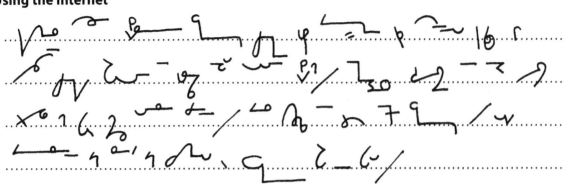

Exercise 20.5

Read the following passage and then prepare for dictation.

Semi-final football match

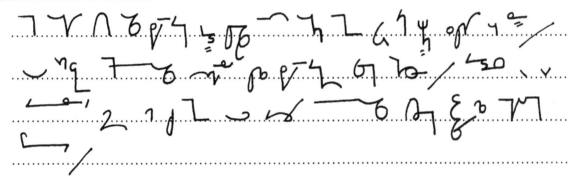

Revision exercise 1

Write the following words in Teeline:

Unit 3 Additional Teeline characters

Letters CH

cheer ....   church ....   teacher ....   patch ....

Letters WH

when ....   whom ....   whip ....   wham ....

Letters TH

them ....   then ....   cloth ....   path ....

Letters SH

should ....   show ....   rush ....   push ....

Vowels

an ....   edge ....   is ....   old ....

hero...................   agenda ....   aim ....   toe ....

ship ....   shop ....   shape ....   sheep ....

Unit 4 Letter S

was ....   sob ....   seems ....   sugar ....

sun ....   museum ....   caused ....   resume ....

rest ....   past ....   desire ....   haste ....

house ....   sap ....   raise ....   serious ....

zoom ....   zip ....   razor ....   magazine ....

season ....   suspend ....   houses ....   basis ....

Unit 5 Letters T and D

tell ....   took ....   atom ....   stab ....

dive ....   deem ....   idol ....   said ....

tap ....   stop ....   tiger ....   stagger ....

bite ....   rabbit ....   bed ....   robbed ....

sent ....   mast ....   send ....   missed ....

tight ....   total ....   tied ....   waited ....

date ....   details ....   deed ....   divided ....

ride ....   right ....   hard ....   hurt ....

tough ....   deaf ....   foot ....   food ....

kid ....   kit ....   task ....   risk ....

cut ....   could ....   cooked ....   cooker ....

Revision exercise 2

Write the following words in Teeline:

Unit 6 Word groupings

....

we shall   you will   I must   to see   we should have   as soon as

ABLE/ABLE TO

....

we are able to   I am able to   he is able to   are you able to

BE/BEEN

....

to be   may be   could be   has been   you have been

THE

....

at the   of the   that the   is the   we have the   from the

....

and the   with the   to the   if the   at the same time

FACT

....

in fact   the facts   these facts   the fact that

WOULD

....

would you   would have   would be   would we   would we be able to

....

you would   I would   we would   it would   I would like   they would

Unit 7 Letters Y and I; letters G or J

-AY and -EY at the end of a word

lay ....   bay ....   obey ....   café....................

hay ....   pay ....   may ....   key ....

I and Y at the end of a word

my ....   lie ....   sigh....................   guy ....

many ....   any ....   lady....................   sorry ....

Y in the middle of a word

system....................   lawyer....................

-LY at the end of a word

sadly ....   nearly ....   badly ....   quickly ....

-OY in a word

boy ....   toys ....   loyal ....   royalty ....

Letters G or J

major ....   enjoy ....   injure ....   injury ....

Unit 8 Letter L

leave ....   call ....   laid ....   stale ....

luck ....   lag ....   lime....................   lane ....

pile ....   pillow ....   gale....................   jail ....

hill ....   meal ....   nail ....   jelly....................

pilot....................   pulled ....   halt ....   hold ....

Revision exercise 2

PL blend

please ....   ply ....   play ....   plot.......................

plan ....   plug ....   plum ....   place ....

apple ....   apply ....   supple ....   supply ....

reply ....   ample ....   display ....   duplicate ....

Words ending -ALITY, -ELITY, -ILITY, -OLITY

quality ....   jollity ....   agility ....   fidelity ....

Words ending -ARITY, -ERITY, -ORITY, -URITY

charity ....   temerity ....   priorities ....   security ....

Revision exercise 3

Write the following words in Teeline:

Unit 9 Use of vowels

Full vowels are: A .... E .... I .... O .... U ....

Indicators are: A ..../......... E ..../......... I ..../......... O .... U ....

(show direction of writing)

Letter A

admit .... adult .... agenda .... rota ....

answer .... media .... avail .... away ....

axe .... art .... arm .... army ....

arrive .... arrival .... arise .... arrest ....

Words beginning AUTO-, AFTER- and AIR-, AER- or ARCH-

automatic .... automatically .... automated...........................

afterthought .... aftercare .... aerospace ....

airgun .... archer .... architect............................

Letter E

edit .... energy .... elm .... see ....

knee .... pea .... epic .... equip ....

Letter I

ignore .... idiot................... lie .... tie ....

ill .... illegal .... Ivor .... ivory ....

Letter O

oak ....   olive ....   hello ....   ego ....

orange ....   ordeal ....   organ ....   original ....

O blended with N and O blended with M

on ....   online ....   onset ....   lesson ....

omit ....   omen ....   move ....   room ....

Words beginning OVER-

overtake ....   overcoat ....   overlook ....

Letter U

umpire ....   ugly ....   unit ....   ultimate ....

up ....   us ....   utmost ....   utilise ....

clue ....   issue ....   sue ....   tissue ....

Europe ....   urge ....   urn ....   urgent ....

Words beginning UPPER-, ULTRA- and UN-

upper-cut ....   uppermost ....   upper-class ....

ultrasound ....   ultraviolet ....   ultrasonic ....

unhappy ....   unsafe ....   unrest ....

R followed by M

ram ....   remain ....   rim ....   room ....

Unit 10 Use of vowel indicators as word endings

Vowel indicators as word endings

sing ....   rings ....   tingle ....   binge ....

sang ....   gangs ....   hanged ....   range ....

song ....   wronged ....   longing ....   sponge ....

sung ....   rungs ....   younger ....   lunge ....

length ....   lengthen ....   lengthy ....   challenge ....

Extending vowel indicators as word endings

sink ....   shrinking ....   winked ....   stinker ....

sank ....   banking ....   tanks ....   blanket ....

plonk ....   honked ....   monks ....   donkey ....

junk ....   bunker ....   hunks ....   chunky ....

Revision exercise 4

Write the following words in Teeline:

Unit 11 Letter F

face....................	fun	fake	five....................
for	first	frill	fraud ....
rough	refuse	surf.....................	surfing ....
refer	refresh	fly	follow.................
fame....................	few	wife	feeble ....
fibre	chief....................	knife	enough ....

Words ending -FUL

careful	hopeful	useful	cheerfully ....

Words ending -FULNESS

usefulness	forgetfulness	carefulness ....

Words ending -LESSNESS/-LOUSNESS

helplessness	thoughtlessness	callousness ....

Words beginning or ending with SELF

selfish	selfless	myself	itself ....
yourselves		themselves	

Unit 12 X blends, N blends and V blends

X blends

excuse ....   examine ....   wax ....   mix ....

expert ....   exhaust ....   hoax ....   annexe ....

exclaim ....   exclude ....   excel ....   excellent ....

N blends

navy ....   novel ....   van...................   vandal ....

ran.....................   coroner ....   month ....   anthem ....

win ....   owner ....   now...................   newt...................

V blends

pave...................   pivot ....   heave ....   behave ....

Words beginning EV- and EVER-/EVERY-

eve ....   evade ....   everlasting ....   everyone ....

Words ending -EVER

whatever ....   whenever ....   whichever ....   never ....

Unit 13 LR, MR and WR blends; MB and PB blends

LR blend

learn...................   salary..................   paler ....   earlier.................

MR blend

more ....   summer ....   customer ....   memory ....

WR blend

work ....   lower ....   fewer ....   viewer.....................

MB blend

mob ....   mobile.....................   bomb ....   bump ....

PB blend

public ....   republic ....   publish ....   puberty ....

Unit 14 The R principle – BR, CR, GR and PR

BR

break ....   brown ....   abbreviate ....   bridge ....

CR

crime ....   credit ....   crown ....   crave ....

GR

grime ....   grown ....   agreed ....   regret ....

PR

product ....   prowl ....   propose ....   apprehend ....

Revision exercise 5

Write the following words in Teeline:

Unit 15 Words ending –SHUN, –SHL, –SHIP and –SHUS

Words ending -SHUN

magician ....   mention ....   occasion ....   ocean ....

oceans ....   fashionable ....   sufficient ....   occasional ....

patience ....   impatience ....   efficiency ....   sufficiency ....

Words ending -SHL

special ....   marshals ....   essentially ....   speciality ....

Words ending -SHIP

hardship ....   friendship ....   relationships ....   battleships ....

Words ending -SHUS

delicious ....   precious ....   anxious ....   cautious ....

Unit 16 T and D blends

TR/DR blend

trip ....   attract ....   reporter ....   history ....

drive ....   address ....   dark ....   moderate ....

TN/DN blend

tin ....   standing ....   retains ....   entertain ....

done ....   suddenly ....   gardens ....   redundant ....

TRN/DRN blend

train ....   returned ....   draining ....   modern ....

THR blend

other ....   mother ....   another ....   rather ....

throw ....   through ....   threat ....   thread ....

CTR blend

cater ....   collectors ....   factory ....   lecturer ....

Words beginning TRANS-

transport ....   transmit ....   transfer ....   transpire ....

Words beginning UNDER-

understand ....   undermine ....   undertake ....   underway ....

Words ending -NESS

sweetness ....   neatness ....   sadness ....   lightness ....

Unit 17 Letter C

CM blend

camp ....   scheme ....   welcome ....   common ....

Words beginning ENCOM-/INCOM-

encompass ....   income ....   incompetent ....   incomplete ....

Words beginning RECOM-

recompense ....   recommend ....   recommendation ....

Words ending -NCE

dance ....   announced ....   balances ....   agency ....

Words ending -NCH

lunch ....   punched ....   benches ....   munching ....

CN blend

can ....   cinema ....   taken ....   inconsiderate ....

CNV blend

canvas ....   convex ....   convert ....   conventional ....

Revision exercise 6

Write the following numbers and words in Teeline:

Unit 18 Numbers, currencies, measurements, abbreviations and colloquialisms

Numbers and currencies

| 1 | 7 | 400 | 5000 | 2,000,000 | 300,000,000 | 5,000,000,000 |

¾ 5% £4 £300 €50 $20 $400 2003 1956 21st century

Measurements

15 grams   5 kilograms   25 metres   8 centimetres

4000 kilometres   40 millimetres   15 litres   7 millilitres

Abbreviations

MP .... NHS .... United States of America ....

Days/Months

Wednesday .... Saturday .... January .... November ....

Colloquialisms

I'm .... I am .... it's .... it is ....

Unit 19 More word endings

-ABLE, -ABILITY ....

table   stables   disabled   reasonably   availability

-IBLE, -IBILITY ....

sensible   visibility   legibly   terribly

-EB(B)LE, -EBEL ....

rebel   pebbles   pebbly   trebling

-OB(B)LE, -OUBLE, -OBILITY ....

hobble   troubled   doubles   nobility

-UB(B)LE, -UBILITY ....

stubble   bubbles   bubbly   solubility

-WOOD, -WORD, -WARD, -WIDE ....

plywood   crosswords   rewarded   worldwide

....

look forward   move forward

-MENT ....

management   garments   experimental   sentimentally

-AVITY, -EVITY ....

gravity   cavity   brevity   longevity

-TIVITY ....

activity   productivity   relativity   sensitivity

-OVER ....

hangover   changeover   takeover   flyover

-JECT ....

subject   injects   rejected   objective

-GRAM ....

monogram   diagrams   programming   programmer

-GRAPH ....

paragraph   autographs   photographer   geography

-OLOGY, -ALOGY ....

biology   meteorology   sociology   genealogy

-OLOGICAL, -ALOGICAL ....

biological   psychological   genealogical

-OLOGIST ....

biologist   sociologist   zoologist

Unit 20 More word beginnnigs

INC-, ENC- ....

include   increase   encourage   encroach

INS-, INT- ....

insure   instance   interest   interfere

SUPER- ....

supervise   supersede   superhuman   supernatural

ABOVE- ....

above-named   above-average   above-mentioned

MULTI- ....

multiply   multitude   multi-storey   multi-coloured

NATION-, NON- ....

national   nationwide   nonsense   non-stop

SEMI- ....

semi-final   semi-detached   semi-conscious   semi-circle

ANTI-, ANTE-, ANTA- ....

anticipate   antiquated   ante-room   antagonise

ELECTRI-, ELECTRO- ....

electrify   electrocute   electrode

MAGNA-, MAGNE-,
MAGNI-, MAGNO- ....

magnanimous   magnetic   magnificent   magnolia

MICRO- ....

microphone   microwave   microscope   microfilm

Common words represented by letters A–M

	4th attempt	3rd attempt	2nd attempt	1st attempt	cover or ← fold
able	....	....	....	....	......Λ....
able to	....	....	....	....	......Λ....
ability	....	....	....	....	......Λ....
after	....	....	....	....	......Λ....
a	....	....	....	....	......\
at	....	....	....	....	....
be	....	....	....	....	......6....
been	....	....	....	....	......6....
once	....	....	....	....	......ϲ....
offence	....	....	....	....	......ϲ....
day	....	....	....	....	......—....
do	....	....	....	....	......—....
electric	....	....	....	....	......L....
England	....	....	....	....	......L̲....
ever	....	....	....	....	......ı....
every	....	....	....	....	......ı....
from	....	....	....	....	......ρ
gentleman	....	....	....	....	......ʔ
go	....	....	....	....	......ʔ
he	....	....	....	....	......ı
I/eye	....	....	....	....	......ʋ....
kind	....	....	....	....	......<....
knowledge	....	....	....	....	......<....
like	....	....	....	....	......<....

	4th attempt	3rd attempt	2nd attempt	1st attempt	cover or ← fold
letter	....	....	....	....	....(....
local	....	....	....	....	....(....
me	....	....	....	....	..⌢..
time	....	....	....	....	⌒ ....

Common words represented by letters N–Y

	4th attempt	3rd attempt	2nd attempt	1st attempt	cover or ← fold
and	....	....	....	....	......ŋ.........
began	....	....	....	....	......η......
begin	....	....	....	....	......η......
begun	....	....	....	....	......η˜......
of	....	....	....	....	....
page	....	....	....	....	......	......
pence	....	....	....	....	......	......
police	....	....	....	....	......	......
question	....	....	....	....	...ʊ̸......
equal	....	....	....	....	...ʊ̸......
are	....	....	....	....	...../......
south	....	....	....	....	......o......
southern	....	....	....	....	......o̲......
to	....	....	....	....	....
you	....	....	....	....	......ʋ......
very	....	....	....	....	......v......
have	....	....	....	....	......ʔ......
village	....	....	....	....	......v......
versus	....	....	....	....	......v......
evidence	....	....	....	....	......v......
evident	....	....	....	....	......v......
we	....	....	....	....	......‿......
accident	....	....	....	....	....x......
your	....	....	....	....	....u......

Special outlines

	4th attempt	3rd attempt	2nd attempt	1st attempt	cover or ← fold
account	....	....	....	....	....
chairman	....	....	....	....	
company	....	....	....	....	....
each	....	....	....	....	
etcetera	....	....	....	....	
much	....	....	....	....	
o'clock	....	....	....	....	
representative	....	....	....	....	....
shall	....	....	....	....	....
such	....	....	....	....	
that	....	....	....	....	....
the	....	....	....	....	
they	....	....	....	....	....
what	....	....	....	....	
which	....	....	....	....	....
with	....	....	....	....	
within	....	....	....	....	....
without	....	....	....	....	

Special outlines

	4th attempt	3rd attempt	2nd attempt	1st attempt	cover or ← fold
also	....	....	....	....	....
always	....	....	....	....	....
because	....	....	....	....	....
business	....	....	....	....	....
businesses	....	....	....	....	....
hospital	....	....	....	....	....
husband	....	....	....	....	....
success	....	....	....	....	....

Special outlines

	4th attempt	3rd attempt	2nd attempt	1st attempt	cover or ← fold
different	....	....	....	....	....
difficult	....	....	....	....	....
establish	....	....	....	....	....
immediate	....	....	....	....	....
incident	....	....	....	....	
particular	....	....	....	....	....
residents	....	....	....	....	....
respect	....	....	....	....	....
today/to do	....	....	....	....	
together	....	....	....	....	
witness	....	....	....	....	....
witnesses	....	....	....	....	....

Special outlines

	4ᵗʰ attempt	3ʳᵈ attempt	2ⁿᵈ attempt	1ˢᵗ attempt	cover or ← fold
club	....	....	....	....	....
clubs	....	....	....	....	....
job	....	....	....	....	....
jobs	....	....	....	....	....
absolute	....	....	....	....	....
absolutely	....	....	....	....	....
city	....	....	....	....	....
difficulty	....	....	....	....	....
immediately	....	....	....	....	....
necessary	....	....	....	....	....
obvious	....	....	....	....	....
obviously	....	....	....	....	....
particularly	....	....	....	....	....
regular	....	....	....	....	....
regularly	....	....	....	....	....

Special outlines

	4th attempt	3rd attempt	2nd attempt	1st attempt	cover or ← fold
child	....	....	....	....	....
employ	....	....	....	....	....
guilty	....	....	....	....	....
people	....	....	....	....	....
area	....	....	....	....	....
English	....	....	....	....	....
equivalent	....	....	....	....	....
hand	....	....	....	....	....
individual	....	....	....	....	....
member	....	....	....	....	....
only	....	....	....	....	....
opportunity	....	....	....	....	....
or	....	....	....	....	....
ought	....	....	....	....	....
remember	....	....	....	....	....

Special outlines

	4th attempt	3rd attempt	2nd attempt	1st attempt	cover or ← fold
anything	....	....	....	....	....
arrange	....	....	....	....	....
enclose	....	....	....	....	....
enclosed	....	....	....	....	....
enclosure	....	....	....	....	....
everything	....	....	....	....	....
nothing	....	....	....	....	....
something	....	....	....	....	....

Special outlines

	4th attempt	3rd attempt	2nd attempt	1st attempt	cover or ← fold
before	....	....	....	....	
fortunate	....	....	....	....	
frequent	....	....	....	....	
half	....	....	....	....	
inform	....	....	....	....	
manufacture	....	....	....	....	
perfect	....	....	....	....	
perfectly	....	....	....	....	
profit	....	....	....	....	
referee	....	....	....	....	
reference	....	....	....	....	
satisfactory	....	....	....	....	
successful	....	....	....	....	
telephone	....	....	....	....	
therefore	....	....	....	....	
unfortunately	....	....	....	....	

Special outlines

	4th attempt	3rd attempt	2nd attempt	1st attempt	cover or ← fold
advantage	....	....	....	....	
approximately	....	....	....	....	
disadvantage	....	....	....	....	
enthusiasm	....	....	....	....	
enthusiastic	....	....	....	....	
exchange	....	....	....	....	
exist	....	....	....	....	
expect	....	....	....	....	
experience	....	....	....	....	
however	....	....	....	....	
inexperience	....	....	....	....	
involve	....	....	....	....	
maximum	....	....	....	....	
minimum	....	....	....	....	
nevertheless	....	....	....	....	
next	....	....	....	....	
north	....	....	....	....	
several	....	....	....	....	
vandalism	....	....	....	....	

Unit 13: Drill exercise 11
Special outlines

	4th attempt	3rd attempt	2nd attempt	1st attempt	cover or ← fold
employer	....	....	....	....	
hour	....	....	....	....	
jury	....	....	....	....	
landlord	....	....	....	....	
mayor	....	....	....	....	
motorway	....	....	....	....	
our	....	....	....	....	
public	....	....	....	....	
remark	....	....	....	....	
tomorrow	....	....	....	....	
were	....	....	....	....	
where	....	....	....	....	
worthwhile	....	....	....	....	
world	....	....	....	....	

Special outlines

	4th attempt	3rd attempt	2nd attempt	1st attempt	cover or ← fold
appropriate	....	....	....	....	
important	....	....	....	....	
improve	....	....	....	....	
newspaper	....	....	....	....	
permanent	....	....	....	....	
prejudice	....	....	....	....	
preliminary	....	....	....	....	
prepare	....	....	....	....	
principal	....	....	....	....	
principle	....	....	....	....	
probable	....	....	....	....	
probably	....	....	....	....	
problem	....	....	....	....	
proportion	....	....	....	....	

Special outlines

	4th attempt	3rd attempt	2nd attempt	1st attempt	cover or ← fold
association	....	....	....	....	....
attention	....	....	....	....	....
electrician	....	....	....	....	....
examination	....	....	....	....	....
financial	....	....	....	....	....
identification	....	....	....	....	....
information	....	....	....	....	....
intention	....	....	....	....	....
organisation	....	....	....	....	....
prosecution	....	....	....	....	....
qualification	....	....	....	....	....
social	....	....	....	....	....
society	....	....	....	....	....
station	....	....	....	....	....

Special outlines

	4th attempt	3rd attempt	2nd attempt	1st attempt	cover or ← fold
alternative	....	....	....	....	
children	....	....	....	....	
extra	....	....	....	....	
extraordinary	....	....	....	....	
general	....	....	....	....	
generally	....	....	....	....	
signature	....	....	....	....	
substantial	....	....	....	....	
their	....	....	....	....	
there	....	....	....	....	
yesterday	....	....	....	....	

Special outlines

	4th attempt	3rd attempt	2nd attempt	1st attempt	cover or ← fold
circumstance	....	....	....	....	
circumstances	....	....	....	....	
committee	....	....	....	....	
communication	....	....	....	....	
community	....	....	....	....	
conference	....	....	....	....	
congratulate	....	....	....	....	
congratulations	....	....	....	....	
consequent	....	....	....	....	
convenience	....	....	....	....	
convenient	....	....	....	....	
council	....	....	....	....	
councillor	....	....	....	....	
county	....	....	....	....	
difference	....	....	....	....	
discontinue	....	....	....	....	
discount	....	....	....	....	
importance	....	....	....	....	
inconvenience	....	....	....	....	
inconvenient	....	....	....	....	
insignificant	....	....	....	....	
insurance	....	....	....	....	
recent	....	....	....	....	
recognise	....	....	....	....	

	4th attempt	3rd attempt	2nd attempt	1st attempt	cover or ← fold
recommend	....	....	....	....	
significance	....	....	....	....	
significant	....	....	....	....	
subsequent	....	....	....	....	

Special outlines

	4th attempt	3rd attempt	2nd attempt	1st attempt	cover or ← fold
advert	....	....	....	....	
advertisement	....	....	....	....	
amount	....	....	....	....	....
department	....	....	....	....	
develop	....	....	....	....	
government	....	....	....	....	
impossible	....	....	....	....	
technical	....	....	....	....	
technological	....	....	....	....	
technology	....	....	....	....	
atomic	....	....	....	....	....
electricity	....	....	....	....	
electronic	....	....	....	....	
super	....	....	....	....	
supermarket	....	....	....	....	....

PART 2

Speed development guidelines

Now that you have covered the Teeline theory, you should start building your speed. It is vital, though, that you continually return to the theory to revise, so that you can write outlines quickly and without hesitation.

Try to use your shorthand whenever possible so that you develop confidence in writing and transcribing your own notes. The more you use your Teeline, the more easily and quickly the outlines will spring to mind.

Regular practice is required in order to climb the speed ladder. Concentration is the key to success and you must not let your mind wander for even a second. When taking down dictation from the speed development passages, if you fall behind the speaker and cannot remember what has been said, do not stop writing, but leave a gap in your notes and carry on. Check at the end what you missed out and determine why you fell behind. Practise those words so that next time you attempt the passage, you will not hesitate or fall behind. It will usually take you several attempts to get it right.

As you progress up the speed ladder, do not worry if you find that you stick on one particular speed. This is called a speed 'plateau' and you may become frustrated and feel that you will never progress to a higher speed. At this point you should think positively and be patient. It may take you some time to get off this 'plateau', but with continued regular practice and a positive attitude, you will.

All the following passages are 2 minutes long and have been dictated at three speeds. A selection of outlines precede each passage for you to practise before taking it down from dictation.

When practising these timed dictation passages, the following guidelines may be helpful:

1. Drill the outlines which precede the passage.
   Optional: Cover up the Teeline at the bottom of the page and write the passage neatly and clearly from the longhand. At this stage, you will have time to work out any difficult or unusual words.

2. Start the dictation and take down the passage. Do not stop the recording until the passage ends. If necessary, leave gaps if you fall behind or if you cannot write a word.

3. Transcribe your notes.

4. Check your notes and your transcription with the ones in the book.

5. Drill any outlines which caused you to hesitate or any outlines you got wrong or missed out.

6. Repeat the passage until you can take it down accurately and then try it at the higher speeds.

Passage 1

informed	problems
children	fence
erected	vandalised
security	constructed

New school fence is vandalised

As head of this school, it is my job to[10] keep you informed of any problems that may affect you[20] or your children who come here. Some of you may[30] already know that we have had concerns for some time[40] about the security of our playing field, so we had[50] a fence erected. However, only two weeks after it had[60] been put up, it was vandalised. The fence was constructed[70] of concrete posts and metal panels, so it was a[80] very strong fence. When I saw the damage, I could[90] not believe my eyes. I am very concerned about this.[100]

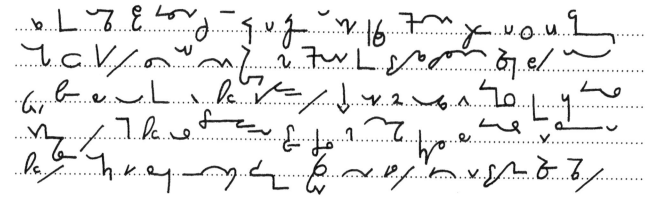

Passage 2

community centre .... 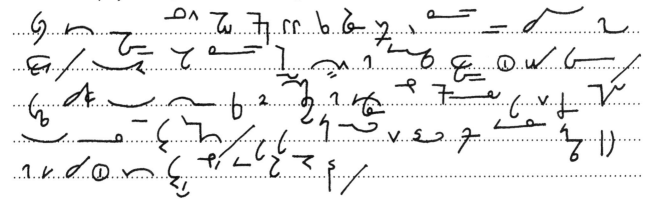 public ....

county council .... project ....

looking forward .... a lot of ....

hundreds of .... at the end of ....

New community centre for town

Ladies and gentlemen, I am delighted to be able to[10] tell you that the county council has at last agreed[20] a start date for our new community centre. Work will[30] start at the end of May and it will be[40] completed one year later. Plans for the centre were made[50] public two months ago and I am pleased to say[60] that hundreds of people have passed through our doors to[70] look at them. A lot of people in the town[80] have shown great interest in this project and I, for[90] one, am looking forward to seeing it all take shape.[100]

Passage 3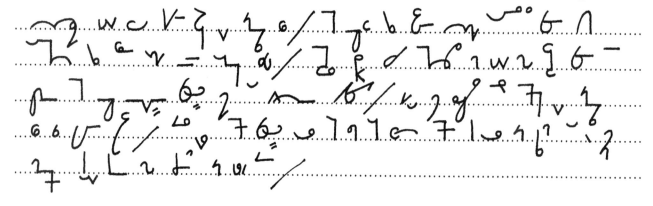

guilty ....

doubt ....

defendant ....

evidence ....

witnesses ....

the facts........................

obvious ....

members of the jury ....

Summing up in case of armed robbery

Members of the jury, you have now heard all the[10] evidence in this case. The defence has called many witnesses[20] but none of them has cast any doubt on the[30] issue. The facts speak for themselves and you have no[40] choice but to find the defendant, David Brown, guilty of[50] armed robbery. I would go so far as to say[60] that the evidence in this case is quite clear. It[70] is obvious that Brown was at the scene of the[80] crime, that he was in possession of a gun and[90] that he would have had no hesitation in using it.[100]

Passage 4 🎧

ladies and gentlemen	professional
in my opinion	thieves
police	over the
area	last few weeks

Lead stolen from chapel roof

Ladies and gentlemen, I am sorry to say that I[10] must share some bad news with you. Last night our[20] chapel was targeted by thieves who stole lead from the[30] roof. A lot of damage has been done and, in[40] my opinion, this is not the work of professional thieves,[50] but it is the work of amateurs. I have, of[60] course, reported this to the police and they have been[70] very helpful. It seems that there have been five incidents[80] of lead thefts from other chapels in our area over[90] the last few weeks. This is a very worrying trend.[100]

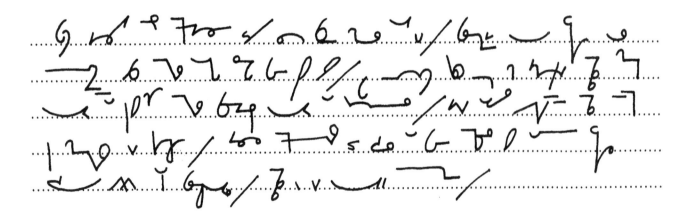

Passage 5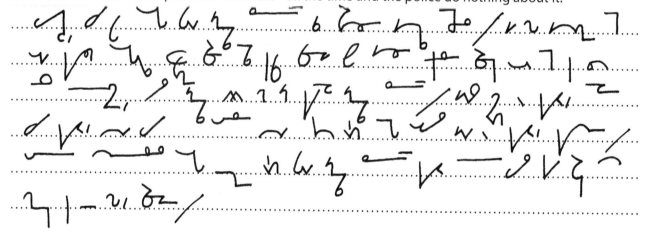

car parking	these days
impossible	only
residents	complained
even	protest

Car parking problems

Car parking for people who live in this street is[10] almost impossible these days. I know I am not the[20] only person who has complained about this problem, but I[30] feel I must protest about the way the police seem[40] to be targeting residents in this area and, in particular,[50] in this street. I have been given a parking ticket[60] for parking my car outside my home even though, of[70] course, I have a parking permit. Other motorists who do[80] not even live in this street park their cars here[90] all the time and the police do nothing about it.[100]

Passage 6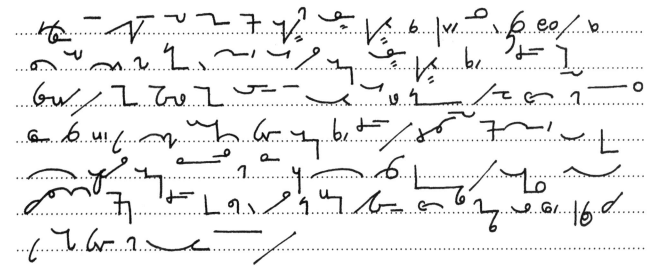

in order to	_ℓ_	as a result of	
success	eo	know	_ɔ_
crime	_ɕ_	mobile	_6_
young	ul	trouble	

Operation West Park

I am pleased to report to you tonight that Operation[10] West Park is proving to be a big success. As[20] some of you may know, I had a meeting with[30] residents on the West Park housing estate at the end[40] of last year. They told us they wanted to work[50] with us in order to reduce crime and trouble caused[60] by young people, many of whom lived on the housing[70] estate. As a result of that meeting, we put more[80] officers on the streets and set up more mobile patrols.[90] We had been aware for some time that the estate[100] had seen a rise in youth related crime and this[110] was causing problems for people who lived and worked there.[120]

Passage 7

understand .... [shorthand]

wonderful .... [shorthand]

down .... [shorthand]

together .... [shorthand]

years ago .... [shorthand]

drink .... [shorthand]

already .... [shorthand]

change .... [shorthand]

Rose and Crown makes way for new housing

I cannot understand why so many people are opposed to[10] the plan to knock down the Rose and Crown pub[20] in Bridge Street to make way for more housing. We[30] all know the pub has been a problem for many[40] years and, in my opinion, this is the right time[50] to get rid of it for good. If you are[60] not already aware of the pub's history, let me put[70] you in the picture. The pub opened in nineteen eighty[80] nine and it was a wonderful meeting place for people[90] who live in this village. Young and old met there[100] several times a week for a drink and a get[110] together. Then, about ten years ago, things started to change.[120]

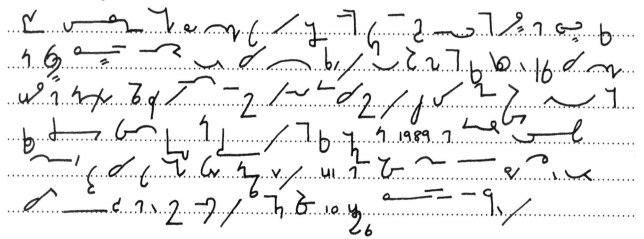

NCTJ Teeline Gold Standard for Journalists

Passage 8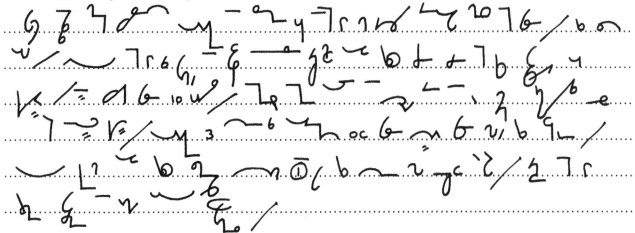

one thousand		more than	
library		in fact	
move		listened	
enquiries		complaints	

Tourist Information Centre to close

Ladies and gentlemen, this is not the first time we[10] have had to stand up to the council and I[20] am sure it will not be the last. As some[30] of you are aware, the council is planning to close[40] the tourist information centre which has been housed inside the[50] public library on Park Road for the last ten years.[60] They say they want to move it to a general[70] enquiries desk at the Town Hall. We have had three[80] meetings with them since last May, but nothing has changed.[90] Our petition, which has been signed by more than one[100] thousand people, has made no difference at all. In fact,[110] the council has not listened to any of our complaints.[120]

Passage 9 🔘

concerned ....

councillor ....

major ....

I would like ....

successful ....

busy ....

campaign ....

to thank ....

Council puts on new bus service for school children

I am pleased to tell you that the council has[10] agreed to put on a new bus service for our[20] children. When my son started at West Side School I[30] was very concerned for his safety. The roads near our[40] estate are very busy and when he walked to and[50] from school he had to cross three major roads. Because[60] of this, I started a campaign to get a new[70] bus service put on and I am delighted to tell[80] you that it has been successful. When I wrote to[90] the council a few months ago my letter was passed[100] to Councillor Jones. He gave a lot of his time[110] to support me and I would like to thank him.[120]

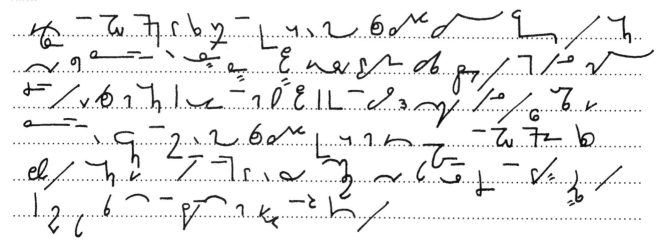

Passage 10 💿

now	discovered ....
project	went ....
evolved	more and more ....
clear	had hundreds of ....

West Marsh Local History Group grows in numbers

It was in nineteen eighty five when we first got[10] together to find out more about our village and the[20] local area. What started out as a small community project[30] has evolved into what we now know as the West[40] Marsh Local History Group. It was clear from the start[50] that our village had hundreds of years of history just[60] waiting to be discovered. I was one of the first[70] members of the Group along with just five others. As[80] the years went on, more and more people joined us[90] and today there are more than two hundred members. At[100] first we used to meet at my house every Sunday[110] night to talk about our plans and share our findings.[120]

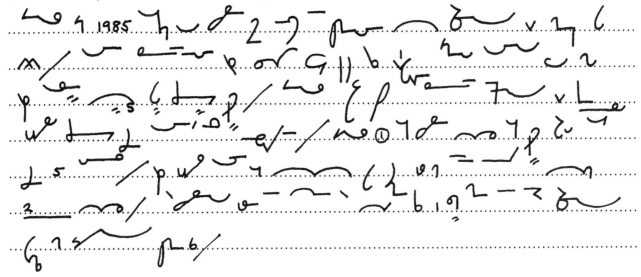

Passage 11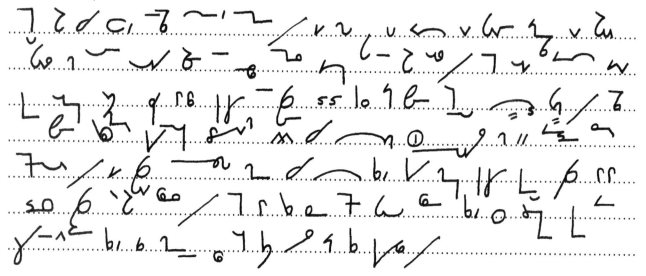

important		put forward	
proposal		county council	
conservation		thank you	
affordable		I think	

Fight against new homes being built

Thank you all for coming to this meeting tonight. I[10] know a lot of you, like me, have lived in[20] this village all your lives and what we are about[30] to discuss tonight is important to all of us. The[40] only item I have put on the agenda is the[50] county council's proposal to build fifty-five houses in the[60] field at the end of Marsh Lane. This field has[70] been part of the conservation area for more than one[80] hundred years and I think it should stay that way.[90] I believe there is no need for more housing here[100] and the proposal put forward by the county council should[110] be blocked at all costs. The council has said that[120] low cost housing or, as they put it, affordable housing,[130] is needed because of the huge rise in house prices.[140]

Speed development

Passage 12

award .... achievement ....

surprise .... celebrate ....

idea .... invited ....

disappointed .... everyone ....

Village of the Year award

It comes as no surprise to me to hear that[10] our village has been chosen as the Village of the[20] Year. This is not the first time we have been[30] put forward for this award but it is the first[40] time we have won it. We came very close to[50] winning two years ago and I know that many of[60] you were disappointed at the time that we did not[70] win, but now that we have made it to the[80] top, we should all feel very proud. It is a[90] wonderful achievement and I am sure that everyone in the[100] village would like to celebrate this success in some way.[110] I think it would be a good idea to have[120] a great big party in the village hall and everyone[130] who lives in the village would, of course, be invited.[140]

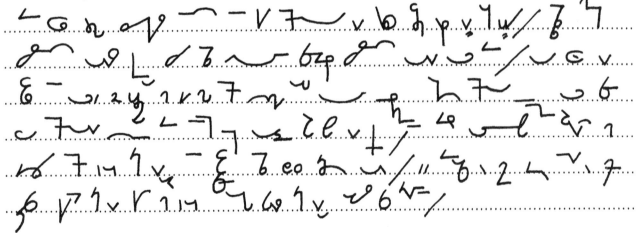

Passage 13

landlords	consequences
town centre	violence
progress	refuse
drunken	too much

Landlords set up Pub Watch Scheme

The town centre is now a much safer place to[10] go than it was two years ago. That is the[20] view of the police, even though two people have been[30] killed in the last year. The police have supported the[40] Pub Watch Scheme and say they are making a lot[50] of progress in the battle against drunken violence. In particular,[60] young people between the age of eighteen and twenty-five[70] now realise that they must behave or face the consequences.[80] In the past, pub landlords and bar staff have had[90] to deal with violence as part of their job, but[100] now they are saying they will not put up with[110] this. They say they have the right to refuse to[120] serve people who have had too much to drink and[130] they will no longer put up with violence or abuse.[140]

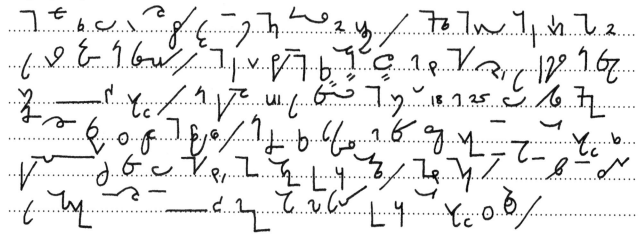

Passage 14

different		children	
English		crisps	
education		teacher	
wonder		grow	

School plans to improve children's diet

Our school is no different from any other, I am[10] sure of that. When I came to work here twenty[20] years ago I was an English teacher. Now, I am[30] the head of the school and I have seen a[40] lot of changes in my time here. I am not[50] talking about the education of our young people. No, I[60] am talking about their diet. Twenty years ago we did[70] not have the same choice of food that we have[80] today. Many of our children like to eat crisps, cakes[90] and bars of chocolate. Many of them never eat a[100] piece of fruit or drink a glass of water. They[110] are used to food that is high in fat and[120] drinks that are high in sugar. Is it any wonder[130] that we are seeing them grow up with health problems?[140]

Passage 15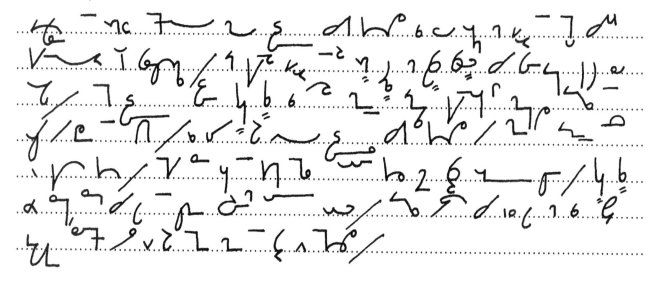

announce .... ɣc ....

shelter .... ς̑ ....

without ....

the facilities .... 𝖳ℓ° ....

none .... ∩ ....

permanent ....

themselves ....

equipped .... 𝖴ɭ ....

Hope House opened as new shelter for the homeless

I am pleased to announce that our new shelter for[10] the homeless is now open and I would like to[20] thank you for your hard work over the last few[30] months. In particular, I would like to thank Ann Jones[40] and Bill Brown for leading the project so well. The[50] shelter, called Hope House, is much needed in this part[60] of the county and the facilities it has to offer[70] are second to none. As you are all aware, shelters[80] for the homeless are not intended to be a permanent[90] home. They are set up to help those without homes[100] get back on their feet. Hope House is a stepping[110] stone for people to find accommodation of their own. It[120] has room for ten people and is fully equipped so[130] that residents have all they need to look after themselves.[140]

Passage 16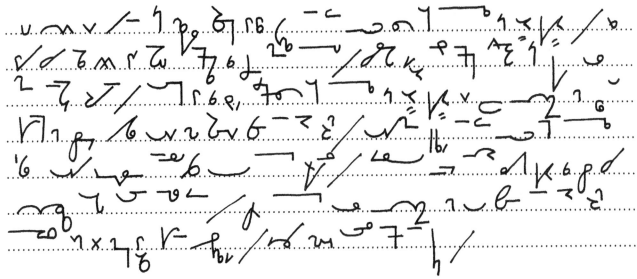

newspaper ....

first of all ....

safety ....

happen ....

proposing ....

I would like ....

alternative ....

responsible ....

members of
the public ....

Health and safety issues over trees

You may have read in the newspapers about the county[10] council's plans to cut down some of the trees in[20] Oak Park. As councillor for this area, I can tell[30] you that this is just not true. First of all,[40] I would like to say that the article in the[50] paper was not totally accurate. What the council is saying[60] is that some of the trees in Oak Park have[70] become damaged and, because of health and safety rules, we[80] have no alternative but to take action. We are not[90] proposing to cut down the trees unless we are advised[100] to do so by our tree experts. It is our[110] duty to make sure the park is safe for members[120] of the public who want to use it. If a[130] tree was damaged, and we failed to take action, there[140] could be an accident and the council would be held[150] responsible. I am sure no one wants that to happen.[160]

Speed development 80/90/100 WPM

Passage 17

at the moment ...... 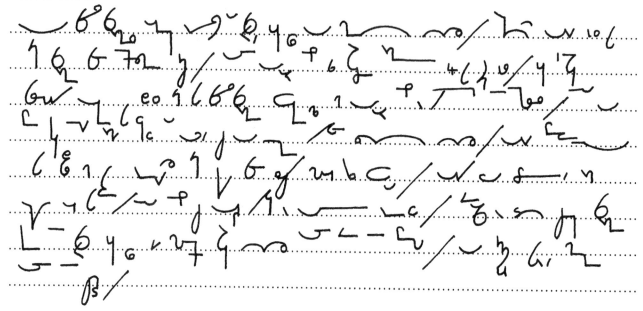   verge ....   brass ....

advertisements ......   audience ......   band ....

competitions ......   breaking ....   recruit ....

Brass band needs more members

Our brass band is on the verge of breaking up[10] because we need more members. At the moment we have[20] ten people in the band, but that is not enough.[30] What we would like to see is at least another[40] four people join us. Up until the end of last[50] year, we had a lot of success in local brass[60] band competitions and we would like to see a return[70] to those days. We cannot hope to have any chance[80] of winning if we do not recruit some more members.[90] We have contacted our local schools and placed advertisements in[100] the paper, but so far no one has come forward.[110] We are now considering an appeal on local radio to[120] see if we can reach a wider audience. It would[130] be a shame if the band had to break up[140] because I know that all the members want it to[150] continue. We enjoy playing and do not want to finish.[160]

Passage 18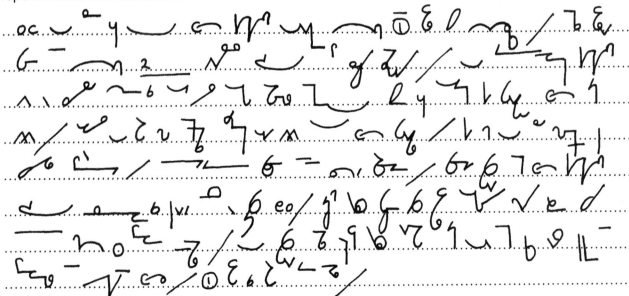

crime ....⌒.........   introduced ....   information..........

one thousand ....①........   arrests ....   approach.........

prepared..........   also ....   all over the country.............

Crime helpline is a success

Since we set up our crime helpline we have had[10] more than one thousand calls from members of the public.[20] These calls have led to more than two hundred arrests[30] in our county so far this year. We introduced the[40] helpline after a series of meetings with residents who told[50] us they were fed up with the high level of[60] crime in the area. Of course, we all know that[70] this is not the only area where crime levels are[80] high and we also know that police forces all over[90] the country are trying their best to do something about[100] it. But I believe the crime helpline in our district[110] is proving to be a big success. Information has been[120] left by callers who are never asked for their name[130] or contact details. We believe this approach has been vital[140] in the way the public have been prepared to contact[150] us to report crimes. One call is all it takes.[160]

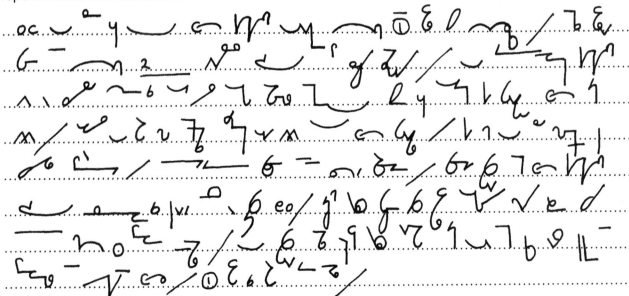

Passage 19

farms .... exciting .... equipment ....

dangerous .... explore .... air ....

often .... as a result of .... under the ....

Farms can be a dangerous place for children

Most children look forward to the long summer days in[10] July and August and the start of their school holidays.[20] They often like to play outside when the weather is[30] good but, as parents, we must make sure that they[40] are safe. Of course, we do not want them indoors[50] playing computer games all day long; we would much rather[60] they were outside in the fresh air being active. But[70] I have to warn you of the dangers of children[80] playing on farms. There are a lot of farms in[90] this area and they may look like exciting places for[100] young people to explore, but they can be very dangerous.[110] Records show that in the last ten years more than[120] thirty children under the age of sixteen have been killed[130] on farms in this country and many more have been[140] seriously injured as a result of accidents. They just do[150] not realise that farm buildings and equipment can be dangerous.[160]

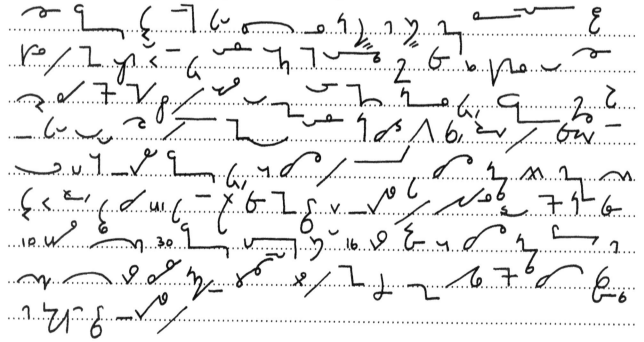

Passage 20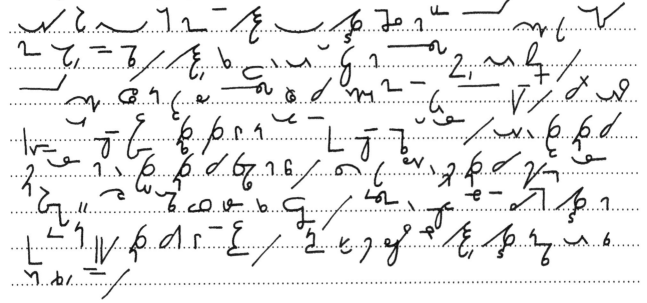

rubbish ....   for example ....   yet ....

recycle ....   general ....   easy thing ....

become ....   although ....   difficult ....

Rubbish must be recycled

We are all aware of the need to recycle our[10] rubbish these days and yet there are many people who[20] are not willing to do this. Recycling has become a[30] way of life and there is no getting away from[40] that. There are many schemes in place so there is[50] no excuse for anyone not to play their part. For[60] example, we have been provided with different coloured bins by[70] the council in which to put different types of waste.[80] We have a black bin for general waste and a[90] blue bin for bottles and cans. Some people also have[100] a green bin for garden waste, although I think much[110] of this could be used as compost. It is not[120] a difficult task to sort the rubbish and put it[130] in the proper bin for the council to collect. In[140] fact, I would go so far as to say recycling[150] rubbish in this way is an easy thing to do.[160]

Passage 21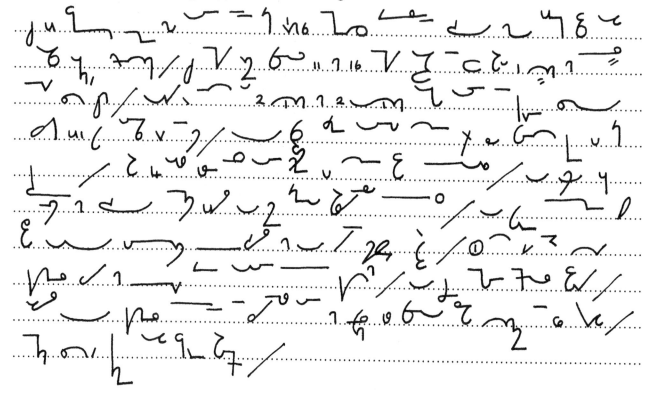

tearaways	discipline	graffiti
welcome	background	havoc
women	expect	all over the place

Tearaways decide to change their ways

If your children do not know what to do in[10] the evenings, they may be interested in our new youth[20] club which will be opening next month. If they are[30] aged between eleven and sixteen, they are welcome to come[40] along every Monday and Thursday to have some fun. We[50] are a team of two men and two women who[60] want to provide somewhere for the young people of this[70] village to go. Our background is not what you might[80] expect so let me put you in the picture. All[90] four of us used to be what you might call[100] 'tearaways'. We grew up together and in our teenage years[110] we got into all sorts of trouble. We played truant[120] from school, we were under-age drinkers and we wrote[130] graffiti all over the place. One time, I took my[140] parents' car and drove it without their permission. We just[150] thought that was clever. Of course, our parents tried to[160] sort us out and discipline us, but we still managed[170] to cause havoc. Then something happened which changed all that.[180]

Passage 22

power		district council		leaflets	
Friday		consumption		room	
secret		o'clock		until	

'Power Down' to save energy

Good evening ladies and gentlemen. I would like to invite[10] you to join me, and thousands of others, in our[20] 'Power Down' day which will take place next Friday. I[30] know that some of you have heard me talk about[40] this before, but I am sure some of you must[50] be thinking what is this all about. Well, let me[60] tell you. It is no secret that we should all[70] be saving energy to help control climate change. This is[80] something which is in the news every day and there[90] is no getting away from it. We, on the district[100] council, would like everyone to think about how they could[110] reduce their own energy consumption and we have come up[120] with the idea of 'Power Down' day. This will take[130] place on Friday the eighth of June, from nine o'clock[140] in the evening until midnight. To give you some ideas[150] on how to go about this, we have produced some[160] leaflets and these are on the table at the back[170] of the room. Please take one on your way out.[180]

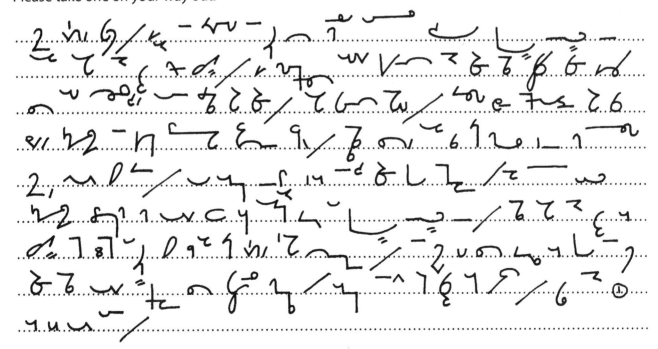

Speed development 90/100/110 WPM

Passage 23

armed .... [shorthand outline]

not only .... [shorthand outline]

police officers .... [shorthand outline]

neighbour .... [shorthand outline]

warranted .... [shorthand outline]

arguing .... [shorthand outline]

incident............ [shorthand outline]

half .... [shorthand outline]

ladies and gentlemen of the press .... [shorthand outline]

Armed police called to incident in Park Road

Ladies and gentlemen of the press, I can now give[10] you some details of the incident which happened last night[20] at a house in Park Road. This incident was attended[30] not only by our police officers, but also by armed[40] officers. You may think that having armed officers at the[50] scene was excessive, but we believe the situation warranted such[60] action. This is what happened. We received a phone call[70] at half past ten last night from a woman who[80] said she could hear screaming and shouting coming from the[90] house next door to where she lives in Park Road.[100] The woman, Mrs Sally Jones, said that she had heard[110] her neighbour, Anne Brown, a single mother with two young[120] children, arguing with a man. This had been going on[130] for almost an hour, but it was only when she[140] heard her neighbour scream, followed by a loud bang, that[150] she decided to call the police. She said that, although[160] this was not the first time she had heard her[170] neighbour arguing with a man, this time it seemed different.[180]

[Shorthand outlines fill the remainder of the page]

Passage 24

criminal ....

I can ....

involving ....

increased ....

fifteen per cent ....

number of ....

as long as ....

evidence ....

reverse ....

Criminal damage is on the increase

I am sure you will agree with me, ladies and[10] gentlemen, that the level of criminal damage in this area[20] is just not acceptable. Our police officers have worked long[30] and hard to bring down the level of crime, but[40] now we are asking members of the public to help[50] us and do their bit. It seems that, in many[60] cases, parents are to blame. They allow their children to[70] go out of the house at night and, as long[80] as they are not under their feet, they just do[90] not care where they go or what they do. I[100] can tell you that over the last two years criminal[110] damage in this area has increased by more than fifteen[120] per cent and in the last year more than two[130] thousand incidents were reported to the police. Of course, I[140] am not saying that children were the cause of all[150] these incidents, but there is evidence to show that the[160] number of crimes involving children under the age of fourteen[170] is rising. We must do something to reverse this trend.[180]

Speed development 90/100/110 WPM

Passage 25

more than	listened	already
urgent	firm	great deal
improve	expert opinion	usual

Council pays business experts to improve town centre

The county council must be the laughing stock of the[10] whole area. For over two years now, the people who[20] live here have been saying that the town centre needs[30] urgent attention in order to attract more shoppers. But, has[40] the council listened? No, it has not. What it has[50] done is pay a great deal of money to hire[60] a firm of business experts to come up with ideas[70] on what they say, in their expert opinion, should be[80] done. The people who live and work here know what[90] should be done and have said so on more than[100] one occasion, but, as usual, the council has not listened.[110] The people who live here have given the council their[120] ideas for free, but, instead of taking notice, they are[130] now paying these business experts to tell us what we[140] already know. Do these so called experts really believe that[150] the things they are suggesting to improve the town centre[160] are things that we have not already told the council[170] about many times before? No, I do not think so.[180]

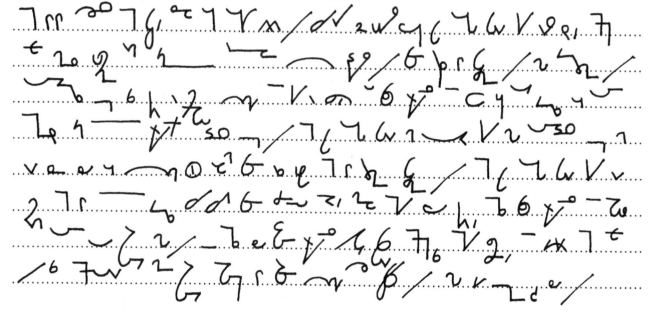

Passage 26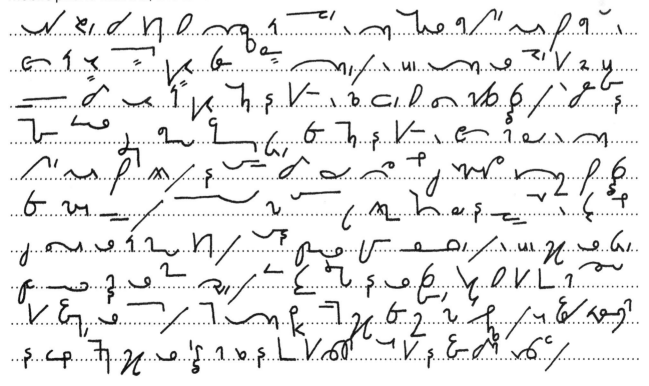

investigation ....   thought ....   unconscious.............

bushes............   emerged ....   someone ....

ambulance ....   moving.........   mobile phone ......

Young girl attacked in Oak Tree Park

We are asking for help from members of the public[10] in tracing a man who was seen running away from[20] the scene of a crime in Oak Tree Park last[30] Saturday morning. A young woman was taking her two-year[40]-old daughter for a walk in the park when she[50] heard a noise coming from some nearby bushes. At first[60] she thought it was just the sound of children playing[70] but then she heard a scream and saw a man[80] running away from the area. She waited for a few[90] moments to see if anyone else emerged from the bushes[100] but no one did. There were no other people around[110] at the time, so she decided to have a look[120] to see if someone was in need of help. What[130] she found was quite disturbing. A young girl was laying[140] face down and she was not moving. It looked as[150] though she was bleeding heavily from her head and most[160] of her clothing was torn. The woman spoke to the[170] girl, but got no response. On closer investigation she could[180] see that the girl was unconscious and, as she had[190] her mobile phone with her, she called for an ambulance.[200]

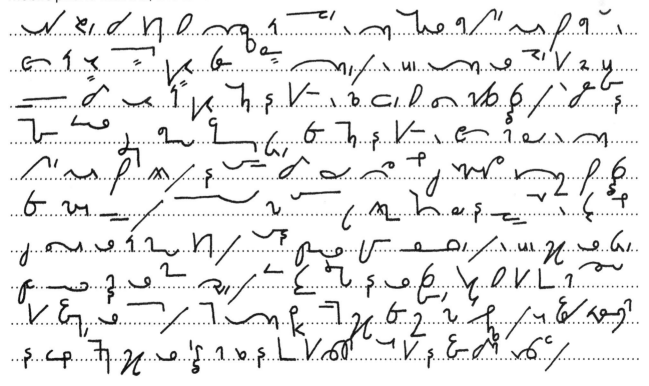

Passage 27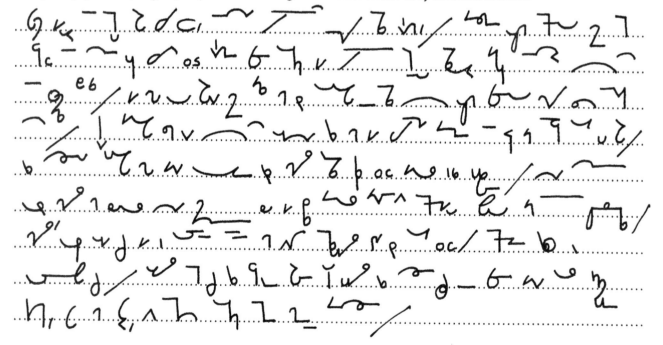

grandmother ..... hands .... social ....

inevitable .... after all .... organise ....

sincerity .... hospital .... footsteps ....

Nurse's retirement dinner

Ladies and gentlemen, I would like to thank you all[10] for coming to my retirement dinner this evening. It is[20] not often that we get the chance to meet up[30] for a social event but when I retire at the[40] end of this week I hope to make more time[50] to organise such things. I know we all have good[60] intentions and say we will do this more often, but[70] we never seem to have the time. However, I will[80] soon have more time on my hands and I certainly[90] intend to keep in touch with you all. As most[100] of you will know, I have worked as a nurse[110] at this hospital since I was sixteen years old. My[120] mother was a nurse and so was my grandmother, so[130] I suppose it was inevitable that I would follow in[140] their footsteps. Nursing was the only job I ever wanted[150] to do and, after all these years, I can say[160] with sincerity that it has been a wonderful job. Of[170] course, the job has changed a lot over the years,[180] as most jobs do, but I have always enjoyed helping[190] people and looking after them when they needed it most.[200]

Speed development 100/110/120 WPM

Passage 28

at the same time .... 　　　　miserable .... 　　　　illness ....

we can .... 　　　　happy .... 　　　　group ....

ourselves .... 　　　　causes .... 　　　　range ....

Fundraising by 'Firm Friends'

Fundraising can be such good fun. That is why we[10] are here today, to have fun and at the same[20] time raise as much money as we can for good[30] causes. We are a group of fifteen women and our[40] ages range from twenty-five to seventy-five. We call[50] ourselves 'Firm Friends'. I started 'Firm Friends' three years ago[60] after I suffered from breast cancer. While I was having[70] treatment for my illness, I was invited to a support[80] group meeting which was run by the hospital. At the[90] time I was feeling quite miserable and I could not[100] imagine a time when I would feel happy and well[110] again. But after attending this meeting, and others like it,[120] I started to see that things would get better. As[130] most of you know, I met Amy Roberts at one[140] of these meetings and since then we have become great[150] friends. We have been through a lot of ups and[160] downs together and we have helped and supported each other[170] through the hard times. It was at one of the[180] support group meetings that I decided to set up 'Firm[190] Friends'. I told Amy and she offered to help me.[200]

Passage 29

traditional ....

business centre ....

developer ....

always ....

eyesore ....

perhaps ....

begin.....................

recently...................

anti-social behaviour ....

Rose and Crown to become a business centre

Thank you all for coming to this meeting. As always[10] there is much to talk about, so let me begin[20] by giving you an update on the old Rose and[30] Crown pub. Most of you know that the pub used[40] to be a thriving business and it was a great[50] place for local people to meet up for a drink[60] and a good night out. It was a traditional pub[70] with plenty of history but it started to have problems[80] when the pub was sold to a young couple from[90] outside the village. It was closed down in two thousand[100] and four after hundreds of complaints from local residents about[110] drug dealings, anti-social behaviour and noise at all times[120] of the day and night. The building was boarded up[130] and, I am sure you will agree, it was an[140] eyesore in the village for a long time. However, the[150] parish council has suggested that the building should be put[160] to some use and opened up again, not as a[170] pub but, perhaps, as a business centre. A developer has[180] recently bought the building and he has told us he[190] will draw up some plans for us to look at.[200]

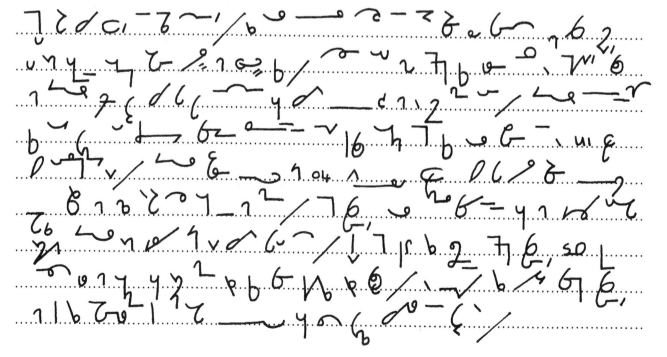

Passage 30

trouble ....

woken ....

neighbour ....

telephoned ....

arrived ....

approach ....

incident ....

wondering ....

in the middle ....

Trouble at Station Road flats

Police were called to the flats in Station Road after[10] a woman, who lives on the top floor, was woken[20] up in the middle of the night by a man[30] who tried to kick down her door. Mrs Rachel Green,[40] who has lived in Station Road for fifteen years, said[50] she had gone to bed quite late on Sunday night[60] and was woken up at about two o'clock when she[70] heard banging on her door. At first she thought it[80] was a neighbour who was in trouble, but as she[90] went to open the door, she heard a man shouting[100] and swearing. She decided it was not safe to open[110] the door and telephoned the police. They arrived within fifteen[120] minutes. By this time the man had started banging on[130] other doors and some of the neighbours had come out[140] of their homes to try to talk to him. It[150] was clear that the man had been drinking and he[160] was in no mood to be reasonable. When he saw[170] the police approach he ran off and the police followed.[180] The whole incident lasted about twenty minutes and Mrs Green[190] and her neighbours were left wondering what was going on.[200]

Examination practice

NCTJ examination passages at speeds of 60 wpm to 120 wpm are available to download from NCTJ's website, www.nctj.com

Now that you have a thorough knowledge and understanding of the Teeline theory, and have started climbing the speed ladder, you should begin to prepare for examinations. The passages on the website above can be used as mock examinations and these will give you a good idea of how close you are to being ready for the real thing. It is important that you prepare as thoroughly as you can in order to ensure a successful outcome in the examination.

The following guidelines are intended to assist you. They are not intended to replace the guidance and advice given to you by your shorthand tutor.

Before the examination

- Aim to arrive in plenty of time before the start of the examination so that you are able to settle in and organise your work station – shorthand notebook ready with a ruled margin, a spare pen or pencil, an English dictionary, etc. Some centres specify the arrival time, so make sure you know what this is.

- Several warm up passages are usually read prior to the examination passage. Take down as many of these as you feel you need to.

- Make sure you are aware of, and adhere to, the rules and regulations of the examination.

The dictation of the examination passage

- Relax and take a few deep breaths. Think positively and be confident that you can do this. You have practised and prepared well for this examination so try not to let nerves get the better of you.

- Write the title of the examination passage in Teeline. The title is not marked, nor is it part of the word count, but it is useful to practise writing these words in Teeline as, very often, the words appear in the passage.

- When the dictation begins, listen carefully to the reader and focus on what is being said. Remember, total concentration is needed and you must not let your mind wander for even a second.

- Do not become flustered if you hear an unusual word. If you are too far behind the speaker and feel you cannot write it down, write the first letter of the word and then move on. When you come to transcribe your notes, context and memory may bring this word to mind. There is little point spending time working out how to write one word at the expense of missing the next few.

Transcription

- Make sure you know exactly how much time you have to transcribe your notes as transcription times differ for each speed.

- Work your way steadily through your notes and do not rush.

- When you have finished, read through it and then check each word against your outlines.

- Count the number of words. Every word missing or added is counted as one error.

- Finally, read through it again to make sure it makes sense.

Each examination you take and pass is worthwhile in terms of achievement and examination experience. Every speed you pass is a step up the speed ladder and with regular practise, commitment and determination, you will soon reach the NCTJ's gold standard of 100 wpm. This qualification, along with the other requisite journalism units, will put you in a good position to gain employment and start working towards the NCTJ's National Certificate Examination (NCE). All your hard work will have been worthwhile as you start your career as a journalist.

Keys to exercises

Unit 1 Introducing Teeline

Exercise 1.4

able	from	do	kind	at	go	be	letter
able to		day	like		gentleman	been	local
ability			knowledge				
after							

he	once	a	electric	I	ever	England	me	time
	offence			eye	every			

Exercise 1.6

and	question	to	you	accident	of	very
	equal					village
						versus
						have

we	evidence	pence	south	your	begin	are
	evident	page	southern		began	
		police			begun	

Unit 2 Writing in Teeline

Exercise 2.1

1. Teeline is fun to learn.
2. Regular practice is needed if you want to reach the standard required.
3. Reporters need to be able to write fast and accurate Teeline.
4. Shorthand is an important skill for a journalist.
5. Practice makes perfect.

Exercise 2.2

Exercise 2.3

blv	pn	rpr	gd/t	ds	mk	grl
lv	hd/t	tl	lvl	mng	dmg	gn

Exercise 2.4

1. I have been to England.
2. You are very kind to me.
3. Police have evidence of your accident.
4. We do like to go to your village.
5. Do you have a question?
6. Will you call a cab to take me home?
7. I believe I will be able to join you in a week.
8. I do like to have home-made cake.
9. I am able to repair your damaged car.
10. He will make time to review your paper.

Unit 3 Additional Teeline characters

Exercise 3.1

cheque	choose	reach	ditch	check	cheap
who	whirl	wham	throw	thug	loath
mash	sham	wish	rush	shave	shrill

Exercise 3.2

1. If you wish to go to church I will go with you.
2. We have had a car accident near the shop.
3. If you have a question, you should see your teacher.
4. The chairman will be here within the week.
5. Which park shall we go to?

Unit 4 Letter S

Exercise 4.1

1. This business has always been a big success.
2. Make sure you go with Susan to the hospital because last time she got lost.
3. I was amazed to hear that the zoo will soon close.
4. They missed the last bus that goes to the village.
5. The chairman has been dismissed from his post.

Unit 5 Letters T and D

Exercise 5.1

1. You must take your dog and rabbit to the vet.

2. She took the test and passed with ease.
3. We waited at the bottom of the road but the bus was late.
4. I have not received the letter you sent to me last week.
5. You must read and write your notes every day.

Exercise 5.2

1. We need some food but I will not be able to go to the shops just yet.
2. He told his teacher he had left his football kit at home.
3. They could have walked to the park but it was difficult because he had hurt his ankle.
4. If you witness a fatal accident you must tell the police.
5. The residents have reported the incident to the police today.

Unit 6 Word groupings

Exercise 6.1

1. <u>I would like</u> to <u>tell you</u> that <u>I have</u> bought some books <u>from the</u> shop.
2. <u>I am sure</u> you <u>could have been</u> at the bus stop <u>with the</u> girls if you had left home <u>at the same time</u>.
3. <u>We shall</u> go <u>to the</u> park <u>as soon as possible</u>. <u>In fact</u>, <u>we shall</u> go today.
4. <u>I have</u> heard <u>about your</u> job <u>from the</u> chairman.
5. <u>I will be able to</u> go <u>to the</u> club with you today.

Exercise 6.2

A visit to the park

<u>We will be able to</u> go <u>to the</u> park together[10] today, <u>but we</u> must <u>leave the</u> house soon because I[20] <u>am sure</u> it will take <u>quite some time</u>. David and[30] Susan <u>will be</u> at the park <u>at the same time</u>.[40]

Exercise 6.3

New job as business representative

<u>I hope you</u> will be able to join <u>this company</u>[10] <u>as a</u> business representative. <u>Of course</u>, if <u>you are not</u>[20] able to, you must tell me <u>as soon as possible</u>.[30] <u>In fact</u>, <u>I would like</u> you to tell me today.[40]

Unit 7 Letters Y and 1; letters G or J

Exercise 7.1

1. <u>We are</u> very busy but <u>we will</u> still go <u>to the</u> café with Amy and Ray today.
2. <u>I am</u> happy <u>to say</u> that <u>I will</u> soon <u>be able to</u> buy a good car.
3. The police have established a good system to allow them to respond to calls without delay.
4. <u>I am</u> sorry <u>to say</u> that <u>we have been</u> told <u>that we</u> must repay <u>all the</u> money.
5. <u>Do you have the</u> key to my house?

Exercise 7.2

1. The judge <u>told the</u> boys they must obey the law.
2. <u>It was</u> obvious <u>that the</u> royal <u>party would</u> not pay the bill.
3. <u>It is</u> absolutely necessary to <u>tell the</u> lawyer all <u>the facts</u>.
4. <u>You will be able to</u> enjoy a good view <u>of the</u> old church if you look beyond the houses.
5. <u>I am sorry</u> to hear <u>that you</u> must go <u>to the</u> hospital immediately because <u>of your</u> injury.

Exercise 7.3

Car accident leads to injury

<u>I am sorry</u> to hear <u>that you have been</u> so[10] badly injured in a car accident. <u>I will</u> <u>visit you</u>[20] <u>at the</u> hospital as soon as <u>I am able to</u>[30] and, <u>of course</u>, Roy and <u>I will</u> <u>visit you</u> regularly. [40]

Exercise 7.4

Boys help old lady

The boys <u>told the</u> old lady <u>that they would</u> carry[10] her bags. This made her very happy so she decided[20] she would give them <u>some money</u> to buy sweets. The[30] boys told her <u>it was</u> not necessary <u>to do</u> this.[40]

Unit 8 Letter L

Exercise 8.1

1. The last person to leave must <u>close the</u> gate behind them.
2. Paul wished his colleague, Jill, good luck with her job.
3. If you climb the hill <u>you will see</u> the lake below.
4. <u>I am sorry</u> to hear that Paul was sent to jail <u>last week</u>.
5. Many old steel mills in England have closed because less steel is in demand <u>these days</u>.

Exercise 8.2

1. If you plan to join the leisure club you should apply immediately.
2. Boys and girls like to play games outside in school holidays.
3. <u>I have</u> seen a splendid display of old books <u>at the</u> city museum.
4. You should eat plenty of plums and apples <u>instead of</u> cakes and sweets.
5. The chairman will reply <u>to your</u> letter <u>as soon as possible</u>.

Exercise 8.3

1. We must make plans to replay the charity football match.
2. <u>It is my pleasure</u> to <u>tell you</u> <u>that these</u> <u>hospital facilities</u> are very good.
3. The plane will take off when the pilot tells his colleagues <u>that it is</u> time to leave.
4. <u>It is</u> obvious <u>that you</u> must look after your health.
5. We employ many people <u>and the</u> goods we supply are of a very high quality.

Exercise 8.4

How to apply to join a club

If you and your <u>child would like</u> to join this[10] club, you should apply immediately. You should send a letter[20] <u>to us</u> and <u>we will</u> reply within a week. Then[30] <u>you will be able to</u> use <u>all the facilities</u> here.[40]

Exercise 8.5

Hospital has good quality of care

<u>You will be pleased</u> to hear <u>that the</u> quality of[10] care <u>at this</u> hospital is very good. <u>As a result</u>,[20] when people have a <u>period of</u> bad health <u>they are</u>[30] happy <u>to be</u> sent here to receive help and support.[40]

Unit 9 Use of vowels

Exercise 9.1

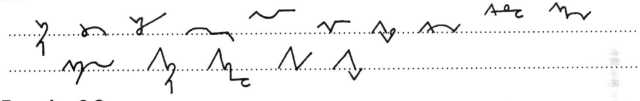

Exercise 9.2

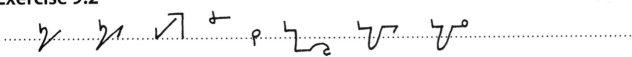

Exercise 9.3

1. <u>Do you have</u> any idea when the artist will arrive <u>as we are</u> eager to meet him?
2. <u>We shall</u> go away with Ray and Alice in May.
3. <u>I would like</u> <u>to see</u> the display of archery this afternoon.
4. Airports are equipped with good security systems <u>these days</u>.
5. Automated machinery <u>should be</u> operated with care.

Exercise 9.4

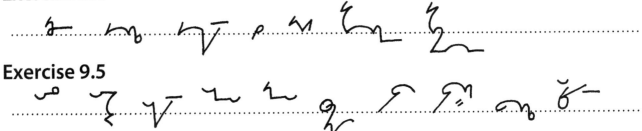

Exercise 9.5

Exercise 9.6

1. If <u>you have</u> an item <u>to be</u> put <u>on the</u> agenda, please tell me <u>as soon as possible</u>.
2. The old lady looked odd in her orange overcoat.
3. The lesson <u>we will have</u> today <u>will be</u> <u>about the</u> Roman army.
4. <u>It is not</u> wise to overtake on a busy road as <u>it could</u> lead to an accident.
5. We <u>visited the</u> Isle of Man on holiday <u>last year</u>.

Exercise 9.7

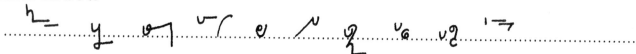

Exercise 9.8

1. The manager <u>of the</u> English football team did his utmost to make sure they remained part <u>of the</u> European league.
2. <u>A lot of</u> people say <u>they are</u> unhappy <u>about the</u> youths who roam <u>around the</u> village late at night.
3. As your house is so big, you ought to let one <u>of the</u> rooms. <u>On the other hand</u>, you may <u>not like</u> this idea at all.
4. Sue and Amy are both upset <u>about the</u> unusual way the issue was handled <u>by the</u> lawyer.
5. <u>I hope</u> you realise <u>that you are</u> always uppermost <u>in my</u> thoughts. <u>After all</u>, <u>you are</u> my only son.

Exercise 9.9

Architect visits city

<u>I am pleased</u> <u>to be able to</u> <u>tell you</u> that[10] Alan Edmonds, an architect, will visit this city in May.[20] He will arrive in plenty of time to go <u>over</u>[30] the plans and also answer any questions you may have.[40]

Exercise 9.10

Visit to Europe

<u>I would like</u> to take this opportunity <u>to say</u> how[10] much I enjoyed my visit to Europe. In particular, I[20] enjoyed the city of Rome and <u>all the</u> splendid views[30] from my hotel room. I usually go to Europe in[40] May.[41]

Unit 10 Use of vowel indicators as word endings

Exercise 10.1

1. <u>I am</u> willing to go <u>to the</u> meeting as <u>many things</u> need <u>to be</u> discussed.
2. If <u>you are</u> going to arrive late, please ring me <u>as soon as</u> <u>you are able to</u>.
3. <u>I will be</u> <u>visiting the</u> manager to discuss my new job.
4. The boys mingled easily <u>with the</u> girls <u>at the</u> party.
5. We must go early <u>to the</u> sales as <u>it is</u> annoying when <u>all the</u> <u>good things</u> have gone.

Exercise 10.2

1. The young boy sang a very good song.
2. If <u>you are</u> unhappy with your job, you should change it and choose <u>something else</u> which <u>will be</u> a challenge.
3. The young child was hungry so she asked if she <u>could have</u> some sponge cake.
4. The police have recovered most <u>of the things</u> <u>that the</u> gang stole <u>from the</u> shop.
5. <u>We have</u> <u>nothing else</u> <u>to say</u> <u>about the</u> meeting but <u>we are</u> very sorry <u>that it was</u> so lengthy.

Exercise 10.3

1. <u>My thanks</u> go <u>to the</u> chairman and his colleagues <u>at the</u> local bank.
2. <u>I will</u> enclose a cheque <u>with the</u> letter <u>I am</u> posting <u>to you</u> today.
3. Junk mail is something we <u>all have</u> to put up with <u>these days</u>.
4. A pink blanket was used to <u>cover the</u> young girl.
5. <u>I think</u> the chunky jumper shrank when <u>it was</u> washed.

Exercise 10.4

Moving house

Moving house is <u>something that</u> many <u>of us</u> do <u>over</u>[10] the years. We <u>all have</u> <u>a lot of</u> belongings and[20] when we move, <u>we are</u> not always willing to throw[30] <u>some things</u> away, <u>but it is</u> obvious <u>that we</u> must. [40]

Exercise 10.5

Junk food is removed from menu

<u>Ladies and gentlemen</u>, this meeting <u>has been</u> called because <u>we</u>[10] are planning to remove junk food <u>from the</u> menu. I[20] <u>think</u> this <u>will be</u> a <u>good thing</u> and although <u>it</u>[30] <u>will be</u> a challenge, <u>we will be</u> <u>making</u> <u>this</u> change[40] <u>as soon as possible</u>.[44]

Unit 11 Letter F

Exercise 11.1

1. You should have enough money if you follow my advice and save a little each week.
2. I am afraid that you will have to defer your surfing holiday because the sea is rough.
3. If you refuse to pay the fine you may face a visit to court.
4. We still have a few houses and flats left for sale.
5. If it is a fine day, Fred will fly his kite.

Exercise 11.2

1. It is a beautiful day and I am feeling very cheerful.
2. Many accidents are caused as a result of carelessness and thoughtlessness.
3. If you suffer from forgetfulness, you should make yourself a list of things to do.
4. Self-employed people are often very motivated to do well in business.
5. I will carry out the survey myself because I was unhappy with the way it was organised last year.

Exercise 11.3

1. It is perfectly satisfactory to telephone me if you would like me to give you a reference for your job.
2. I think it is very selfish of Fred to keep half of the profit from the firm.
3. First of all I would like to thank you for informing me about the fatal car accident.
4. Before you fill in a form yourself, you should refer to the guide on the first page.
5. For the past few weeks I have been thinking about applying for a job at your firm.

Exercise 11.4

A holiday in Africa

Fred and his wife Freda will soon be flying away[10] to Africa for a holiday. They will be staying at[20] a beautiful farm and I am sure Fred will make[30] himself useful by doing a few jobs from time to[40] time. He is always cheerful and usually offers to help.[50]

Exercise 11.5

A visit to the shops

Freda is hopeful that she will be able to visit[10] a few shops before she goes home. She often likes[20] to spend a lot of money on herself, but Fred[30] thinks she is quite selfish and says that it is[40] not at all satisfactory to spend too much money.[49]

Unit 12 X blends, N blends and V blends

Exercise 12.1

1. Please explain why the taxi fare from the nightclub was so expensive.
2. I will excuse you from playing football today, but I expect you to play next week.
3. You should examine goods carefully before you buy them, particularly if they are expensive.
4. We have an exclusive range of luxury goods and they are excellent value for money.
5. It is a good thing for all of us to experience some form of luxury from time to time.

Exercise 12.2

1. I have just finished writing my first novel.
2. The wedding venue was beautiful, but very expensive.
3. The coroner is expected to give his verdict today.
4. The owner of the houses and flats will put up his rent next month.
5. The police have now caught the vandals who smashed my windows.

Exercise 12.3

1. I always invite my friends for a meal whenever I have enough time.
2. I am sure the police will eventually catch the vandals, even though they have no suspects.
3. Nowadays we see a lot of bad behaviour from young people.
4. Several families live in poverty and they have no money whatsoever.
5. Everyone who lives in the north of England will experience heavy rain in the next few weeks.

Exercise 12.4

Vandalism in the town

Nowadays, we hear a lot of news about vandalism in[10] the town. In the last few months several shop owners[20] have reported quite a few incidents involving young people causing[30] havoc. I think the parents of many of these young[40] people are just oblivious to what is going on.[49]

Exercise 12.5

Rise in rent charges

Experts at the town hall have told us that we[10] should expect a small rise in rent charges next year.[20] However, they have explained that they will examine everyone's ability[30] to pay the new rate before it is imposed. Nevertheless,[40] I think we will all experience a rise eventually.[49]

Unit 13 LR, MR and WR blends; MB and PB blends

Exercise 13.1

1. I will be spending my summer holiday in America.
2. More and more people worry about the number of accidents on the motorway.
3. She used the motorway to get to work this morning.
4. It is always worthwhile to learn a new skill.
5. The landlord will collect his rent tomorrow.

Exercise 13.2

Accidents on the motorway

More and more people use the motorway to get to[10] work and we learn of several accidents occurring in our[20] town every day. However, it is the same all over[30] the place because more people use an automobile these days.[40] In my opinion, more people should use the bus to[50] get to work.[53]

Exercise 13.3

Meeting of landlords in the town

Quite a few landlords in the town are planning to[10] meet tomorrow to discuss the new rules that they will[20] have to follow from next year. These rules will soon[30] be published but, in our opinion, it will be worthwhile[40] going along to hear what they all have to say.[50]

Unit 14 The R principle – BR, CR, GR and PR

Exercise 14.1

1. The police have cracked down on aggressive behaviour in our town.
2. If you break the law, you could be sent to prison.
3. I promise we will go to the beach when it is less crowded.
4. I propose to celebrate my birthday next month and I hope you will agree to join me.
5. The bride and groom thanked everyone for giving them such great presents.

Exercise 14.2

1. I regret to inform you that the bridge is closed.
2. The police propose to apprehend the youths who have been causing criminal damage in the area.
3. As you are probably aware, I am not able to promote you even though your work has improved.
4. We have a problem with aggressive young men and they are now causing many people a great deal of worry.
5. *Pride and Prejudice* is a brilliant book and film.

Exercise 14.3

The level of crime is growing

The level of crime is a growing problem not only[10] in this city, but all over the world. More and[20] more criminals are apprehended and sent to prison but this[30] still does not seem to lower the number of crimes[40] that the police have to deal with these days.[49]

Exercise 14.4

Opportunity to improve career prospects

I am very grateful to Mr Brown for promoting me[10] and, even though it will probably create a great deal[20] more work for me to do, it is most important[30] to me that I have been given an opportunity to[40] improve my career prospects at this firm.[47]

Unit 15 Words ending –SHUN, –SHL, –SHIP and –SHUS

Exercise 15.1

1. We have no option but to begin the fashion show as soon as possible because some people are not very patient.
2. I have no hesitation in telling you that education is very important if you want to get a good job.
3. Your suggestion of closing early is a good solution to the problem.
4. If workers are efficient, I think it is important that they are given the opportunity of promotion.
5. Some occasions are very emotional and additional help and support is often required.

Exercise 15.2

1. It is essential that special guests are present at official functions.
2. It is crucial that the police are given all the facts, especially when a fatal accident has occurred.
3. When filling in official forms it is essential that you write your initials clearly.

Exercise 15.3

1. It is good to have close friendships, particularly if you need to talk about your problems.
2. If you want your relationships to be happy, you must work at them.
3. Many colleges no longer have hardship funds to help learners.

Exercise 15.4

1. The chef cooked a delicious meal for everyone.
2. The police want to talk to anyone who saw the vicious attack this morning.
3. You should be cautious where you park your car in a run-down area.

Exercise 15.5

Theft at jeweller's shop

Police are anxious to speak to anyone who was at[10] the bus station this morning. An incident happened which involved[20] the theft of gold, silver and precious gems from a[30] nearby jeweller's shop. Anyone who has any information about this[40] incident should call the police station as soon as possible.[50]

Exercise 15.6

Good qualifications are important

It is important for young people to gain good qualifications[10] if they have any intention of building a successful career.[20] Although they may have financial hardship when they are young,[30] they will eventually go on to earn themselves a good[40] salary, but it is essential that they work hard.[49]

Unit 16 T and D blends

Exercise16.1

1. It is important to drink a lot of water, especially during the summer.
2. It is not wise to drink and drive. It is better to travel by bus.
3. A reporter usually writes stories about news and events in a particular district.
4. Many young people like to travel all over the world before starting a job.
5. I always drive straight home from work on dark winter nights.

Exercise 16.2

1. I will be attending a meeting in London next week.
2. If you think you may be made redundant, you should start looking for another job.
3. The boy's mother and father did not attend the parents' evening at school.
4. The old factory will close to make way for a modern one to be built in its place.
5. Make sure you go through all your old clothes before you throw them away.

Exercise 16.3

1. More than half of the trains on the London Underground do not run on time.
2. Some young children have tantrums when they transfer from one school to another.
3. As a matter of fact, the number of homeless people in London is growing.
4. In order to cater for young children, many restaurants now have an alternative menu.
5. If you witness an accident, you must leave your name and address with the police.

Exercise 16.4

Local authority improves leisure facilities

The local authority has done a lot over the years[10] to try to improve leisure facilities for children. There are[20] now a lot of modern parks which have well-maintained[30] gardens and these attract many visitors, particularly mothers and fathers[40] with their young children, during the school holidays.[48]

Exercise 16.5

Downturn in sales

Traders in the town have been hit by another downturn[10] in sales during the last few months. London, in particular,[20] has had fewer tourists so it is not surprising that[30] sales have dropped. It is hoped that there will be[40] a return to much better sales in the near future.[50]

Unit 17 Letter C

Exercise 17.1

1. I welcome the opportunity to be involved in your campaign.
2. I will accompany you to the new shopping complex tomorrow.
3. Your factory workers are incompetent so I recommend that they are given more training.
4. There are a lot of speed cameras in the city of Cambridge.
5. Most people use a computer to look for holiday accommodation these days.

Exercise 17.2

1. The scheme for the new community housing campaign will be announced next month.
2. It is common knowledge that hotel accommodation is very expensive these days.
3. It is recommended that young people do some work in the community.
4. There will be a lunch party next weekend and it is of vital importance that you come with me.
5. Financial experts have announced that income tax will go up next year.

Exercise 17.3

1. The results of the survey conducted last year have proved to be inconclusive.
2. Candidates taking their driving test must concentrate or they may fail.
3. When applying for a job you must be confident that you can convince the employer to take you on.
4. If I am not mistaken, a visit to the cinema or a concert is considered to be a good night out.
5. It can be difficult to hold a private conversation if you are concerned you might be overheard.

Exercise 17.4

1. There will be a press conference to discuss the recent acts of vandalism in the town centre.
2. We can all recognise the importance of having a healthy lifestyle.
3. It is inconvenient to go to the town centre by car because the car parks are a long distance from the shops.
4. It is a scandal that the county council has taken away such a significant number of jobs from local workers.
5. James Campbell is the councillor for our area.

NCTJ Teeline Gold Standard for Journalists

Exercise 17.5

Park Road flats to be condemned

There has been a campaign to condemn the Park Road[10] flats because they are now considered to be unsafe. The[20] residents' association has contacted the council to recommend that they[30] are knocked down. A meeting will be convened to consider[40] all the options but I can assure you that something[50] will be done by the end of the year.[59]

Exercise 17.6

Youths cause problems in the town centre

There were a lot of problems in the town centre[10] at the weekend when a group of youths became violent[20] and kicked and punched a nightclub owner when closing time[30] was announced. In the circumstances, the police were called and[40] the youths were taken away to face the consequences. These[50] recent events have been very upsetting for everyone concerned.[59]

Unit 18 Numbers, currencies, measurements, abbreviations and colloquialisms

Exercise 18.1

1. I shall be taking five hundred Euros with me when I go to France on Monday.
2. More than eight hundred people were seen on closed-circuit television as they arrived at the bus station on Saturday.
3. There were thousands of spectators at the sports stadium and about two hundred athletes participated in the games.
4. In 2005, the number of car crimes in the UK went up by about fifteen per cent.
5. The two women wanted to lose seven kilograms in weight so they each paid five pounds to join the slimming club.

Exercise 18.2

Collection to buy gifts for teachers

I have collected two hundred pounds from twenty people in[10] my class so that I can buy gifts for two[20] of our teachers who are moving to the United States[30] of America. They joined our school in September two thousand[40] and three. They have been here for five years and[50] there will be a leaving party for them on Saturday.[60]

Unit 19 More word endings

Exercise 19.1

1. Many sports cars are capable of reaching high speeds and they are reasonably cost effective.
2. In bad weather, when visibility is poor, it is important to drive sensibly.
3. It is possible to collect some lovely pebbles on many English beaches.
4. If there is trouble in an undesirable part of town, the police are usually available to deal with it.
5. These days, it is fashionable for young men to have stubble on their face.

Exercise 19.2

1. I enjoy trying to complete the crossword in my newspaper.
2. I look forward to reading a good book when I am on holiday.
3. The management structure at my firm changes on a regular basis.
4. Conditions of employment are fundamentally the same in most companies.
5. Some experimental work is being done at the moment.

Exercise 19.3

1. I must go to the dentist as I think I have a cavity in my tooth.
2. There are a lot of good activities for young people in this town.
3. The management has announced that there might be a takeover bid for the company next month.
4. Productivity has gone up by fifteen per cent.
5. A goal was scored in the last minute and then the game was all over.

Exercise 19.4

1. I have no objection to my son studying extra subjects at school if he has time.
2. I will record the television programme for you if you are going out tonight.
3. The photographer took some wonderful pictures at the wedding.
4. The only subject I did not enjoy at school was biology.
5. The government says it is impossible for them to give an additional amount of money to the National Health Service.

Exercise 19.5

Eating sensibly

Most people try to eat sensibly these days, although a[10] lot of young people do tend to nibble in between[20] meals. A statement issued by the Department of Health has[30] said that healthy eating programmes will be implemented in all[40] schools as soon as possible. I do hope that parents[50] will not object to these plans being put in place.[60]

Exercise 19.6

Advertisement in *The Telegraph*

An advertisement for a sociology course at the local college[10] will appear in *The Telegraph* newspaper tomorrow. This is only[20] one of the many subjects that will be on offer.[30] Other courses and activities will be advertised in the next[40] few weeks. It is impossible to estimate how many people[50] will apply, but we are looking forward to a good[60] response.[61]

Unit 20 More word beginnings

Exercise 20.1

1. The supervisor was asked to increase her working hours at the superstore.
2. Students who achieve above-average examination results often inspire others to do the same.
3. The junior assistants were encouraged to apply for promotion.
4. The intruder was apprehended by the police.
5. His approach to the task was over and above what was required.

Exercise 20.2

1. A judge will not stand for any nonsense from young offenders.
2. There is a national shortage of semi-detached houses.
3. A new multi-storey hotel is being built in the centre of the town.
4. I anticipate that a new government will be elected next year.
5. The semi-final of the football match will take place in February.

Exercise 20.3

1. Gas and electricity prices have increased significantly during the past year.
2. I have a magnificent magnolia tree in my garden.
3. Most modern kitchens have a microwave as well as other electrical appliances.
4. You should not operate faulty machinery as you may get electrocuted.
5. The atomic bomb is a very powerful weapon.

Exercise 20.4

Using the Internet

Parents must supervise their children if they use the Internet[10] as a multitude of problems can result if they are[20] allowed to use this technology without supervision. They should be[30] encouraged to take regular exercise and play games outside instead.[40] It is nonsense to assume that children are only interested[50] in sitting in front of a computer all day long.[60]

Exercise 20.5

Semi-final football match

The whole nation will be supporting the English football team[10] when they play in the European semi-final on Saturday.[20] We anticipate that there will be many thousands of fans[30] supporting them both at home and abroad. It should be[40] a very interesting game and if they win I am[50] sure there will be non-stop celebrations throughout the country.[60]

Keys to revision exercises

Unit 3 Additional Teeline characters

Letters CH

cheer .... church .... teacher .... patch ....

Letters WH

when .... whom .... whip .... wham ....

Letters TH

them .... then .... cloth .... path ....

Letters SH

should .... show .... rush .... push ....

Vowels

an .... edge .... is .... old ....

hero .... agenda .... aim .... toe ....

ship .... shop .... shape .... sheep ....

Unit 4 Letter S

was .... sob .... seems .... sugar ....

sun .... museum .... caused .... resume ....

rest .... past .... desire .... haste ....

house .... sap .... raise .... serious ....

zoom .... zip .... razor .... magazine ....

season .... suspend .... houses .... basis ....

NCTJ Teeline Gold Standard for Journalists

Unit 5 Letters T and D

tell .... *(shorthand)* took .... *(shorthand)* atom .... *(shorthand)* stab .... *(shorthand)*

dive .... *(shorthand)* deem .... *(shorthand)* idol .... *(shorthand)* said .... *(shorthand)*

tap .... *(shorthand)* stop .... *(shorthand)* tiger .... *(shorthand)* stagger .... *(shorthand)*

bite .... *(shorthand)* rabbit .... *(shorthand)* bed .... *(shorthand)* robbed .... *(shorthand)*

sent .... *(shorthand)* mast .... *(shorthand)* send .... *(shorthand)* missed .... *(shorthand)*

tight .... *(shorthand)* total .... *(shorthand)* tied .... *(shorthand)* waited .... *(shorthand)*

date .... *(shorthand)* details .... *(shorthand)* deed .... *(shorthand)* divided .... *(shorthand)*

ride .... *(shorthand)* right .... *(shorthand)* hard .... *(shorthand)* hurt .... *(shorthand)*

tough .... *(shorthand)* deaf .... *(shorthand)* foot .... *(shorthand)* food .... *(shorthand)*

kid .... *(shorthand)* kit .... *(shorthand)* task .... *(shorthand)* risk .... *(shorthand)*

cut .... *(shorthand)* could .... *(shorthand)* cooked .... *(shorthand)* cooker .... *(shorthand)*

Revision exercise 2

Unit 6 Word groupings

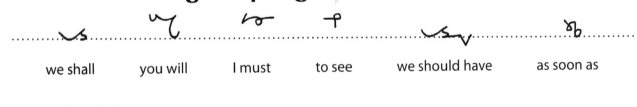

we shall   you will   I must   to see   we should have   as soon as

ABLE/ABLE TO

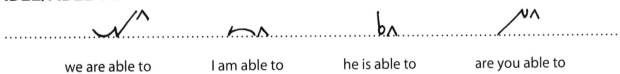

we are able to   I am able to   he is able to   are you able to

BE/BEEN

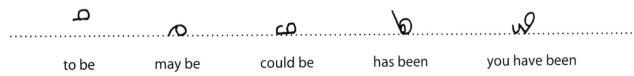

to be   may be   could be   has been   you have been

THE

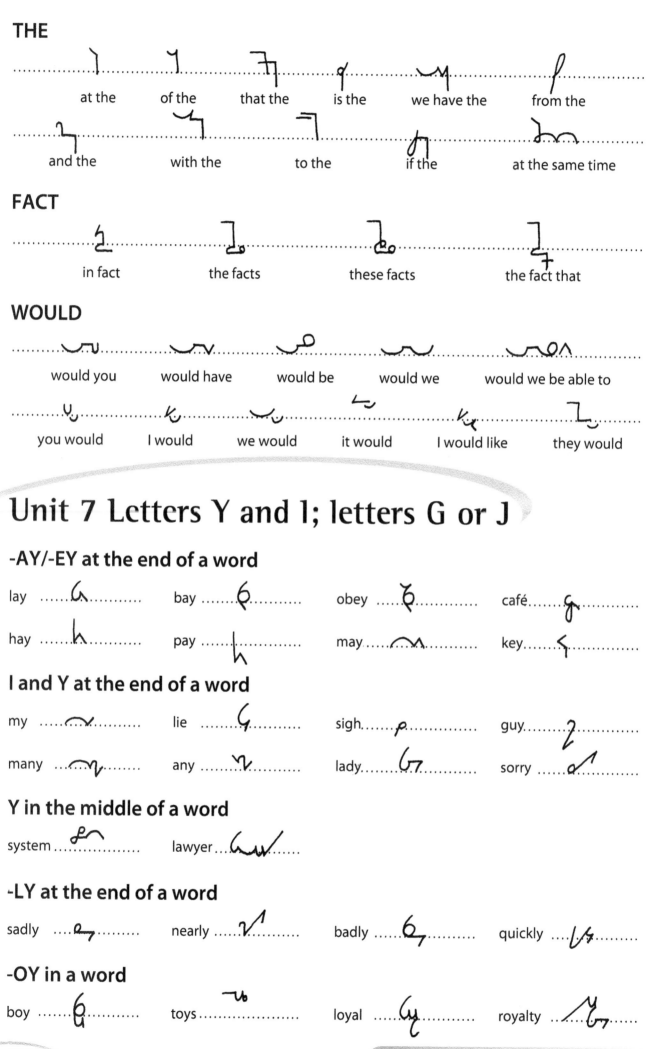

at the   of the   that the   is the   we have the   from the

and the   with the   to the   if the   at the same time

FACT

in fact   the facts   these facts   the fact that

WOULD

would you   would have   would be   would we   would we be able to

you would   I would   we would   it would   I would like   they would

Unit 7 Letters Y and I; letters G or J

-AY/-EY at the end of a word

lay   bay   obey   café

hay   pay   may   key

I and Y at the end of a word

my   lie   sigh   guy

many   any   lady   sorry

Y in the middle of a word

system   lawyer

-LY at the end of a word

sadly   nearly   badly   quickly

-OY in a word

boy   toys   loyal   royalty

Letters G or J

major ....   enjoy ....   injure ....   injury ....

Unit 8 Letter L

Letter L

leave ....   call ....   laid ....   stale ....

luck ....   lag ....   lime ....   lane ....

pile ....   pillow ....   gale ....   jail ....

hill ....   meal ....   nail ....   jelly ....

pilot ....   pulled ....   halt ....   hold ....

PL blend

please ....   ply ....   play ....   plot ....

plan ....   plug ....   plum ....   place ....

apple ....   apply ....   supple ....   supply ....

reply ....   ample ....   display ....   duplicate ....

Words ending -ALITY, -ELITY, -ILITY, -OLITY

quality ....   jollity ....   agility ....   fidelity ....

Words ending -ARITY, -ERITY, -ORITY, -URITY

charity ....   temerity ....   priorities ....   security ....

Revision exercise 3

Unit 9 Use of vowels

Full vowels are: A .... E .... I .... O .... U ....

Indicators are: A .... / .... E .... / .... I .... / .... O .... U ....

Letter A

admit ....   adult ....   agenda ....   rota ....

answer ....   media ....   avail ....   away ....

axe ....   art ....   arm ....   army ....

arrive ....   arrival ....   arise ....   arrest ....

Words beginning AUTO-, AFTER- and AIR-, AER- or ARCH-

automatic ....   automatically ....   automated ....

afterthought ....   aftercare ....   aerospace ....

airgun ....   archer ....   architect ....

Letter E

edit ....   energy ....   elm ....   see ....

knee ....   pea ....   epic ....   equip ....

Letter I

ignore ....   idiot ....   lie ....   tie ....

ill ....   illegal ....   Ivor ....   ivory ....

Letter O

oak ....   olive ....   hello ....   ego ....

orange ....   ordeal ....   organ ....   original ....

O blended with N and O blended with M

on ....   online ....   onset ....   lesson ....

omit ....   omen ....   move ....   room ....

Words beginning OVER-

overtake ....   overcoat ....   overlook ....

Letter U

umpire .... ugly .... unit .... ultimate ....

up .... us .... utmost .... utilise ....

clue .... issue .... sue .... tissue ....

Europe .... urge .... urn .... urgent ....

Words beginning UPPER-, ULTRA- and UN-

upper-cut .... uppermost .... upper-class ....

ultrasound .... ultraviolet .... ultrasonic ....

unhappy .... unsafe .... unrest ....

R followed by M

ram .... remain .... rim .... room ....

Unit 10 Use of vowel indicators as word endings

Vowel indicators as word endings

sing .... rings .... tingle .... binge ....

sang .... gangs .... hanged .... range ....

song .... wronged .... longing .... sponge ....

sung .... rungs .... younger .... lunge ....

length .... lengthen .... lengthy .... challenge ....

Extending vowel indicators as word endings

sink .... shrinking .... winked .... stinker ....

sank .... banking .... tanks .... blanket ....

plonk .... honked .... monks .... donkey ....

junk ....   bunker ....   hunks ....   chunky ....

Revision exercise 4

Unit 11 Letter F

Letter F

face ....   fun ....   fake ....   five ....

for ....   first ....   frill ....   fraud ....

rough ....   refuse ....   surf ....   surfing ....

refer ....   refresh ....   fly ....   follow ....

fame ....   few ....   wife ....   feeble ....

fibre ....   chief ....   knife ....   enough ....

Words ending -FUL

careful ....   hopeful ....   useful ....   cheerfully ....

Words ending -FULNESS

usefulness ....   forgetfulness ....   carefulness ....

Words ending -LESSNESS/-LOUSNESS

helplessness ....   thoughtlessness ....   callousness ....

Words beginning or ending with SELF

selfish ....   selfless ....   myself ....   itself ....

yourselves ....   themselves ....

Unit 12 X blends, N blends and V blends

X blends

excuse ....   examine ....   wax ....   mix ....

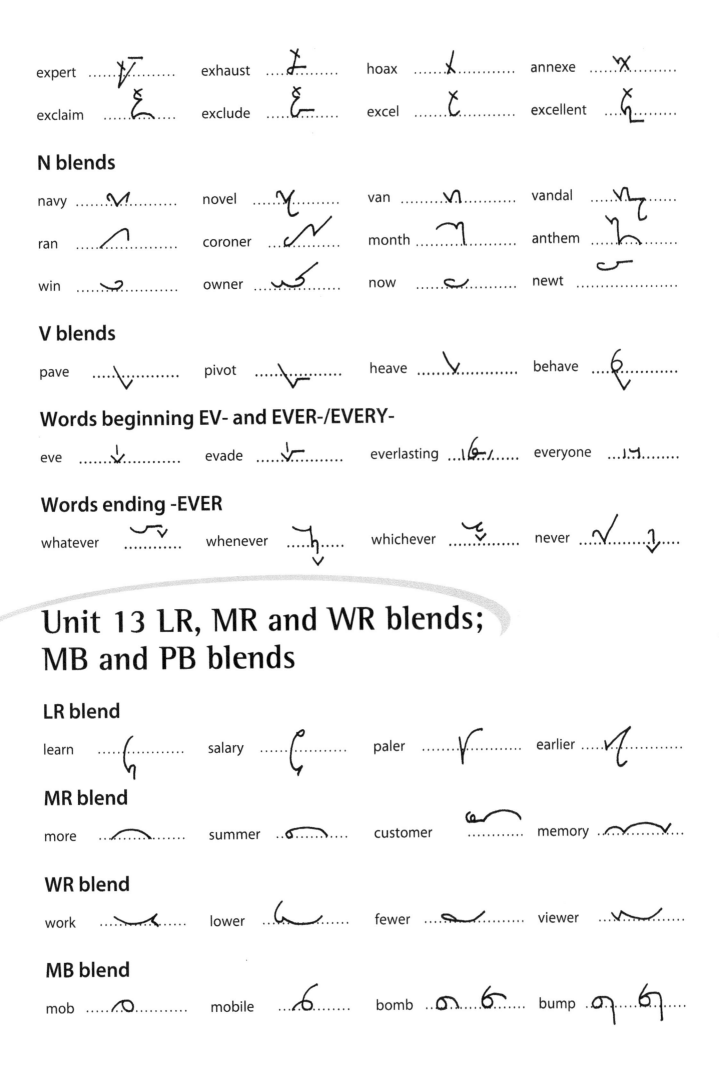

expert .... exhaust .... hoax .... annexe ....

exclaim .... exclude .... excel .... excellent ....

N blends

navy .... novel .... van .... vandal ....

ran .... coroner .... month .... anthem ....

win .... owner .... now .... newt ....

V blends

pave .... pivot .... heave .... behave ....

Words beginning EV- and EVER-/EVERY-

eve .... evade .... everlasting .... everyone ....

Words ending -EVER

whatever .... whenever .... whichever .... never ....

Unit 13 LR, MR and WR blends; MB and PB blends

LR blend

learn .... salary .... paler .... earlier ....

MR blend

more .... summer .... customer .... memory ....

WR blend

work .... lower .... fewer .... viewer ....

MB blend

mob .... mobile .... bomb .... bump ....

PB blend

public .... [shorthand]   republic .... [shorthand]   publish .... [shorthand]   puberty .... [shorthand]

Unit 14 The R principle – BR, CR, GR and PR

BR

break .... [shorthand]   brown .... [shorthand]   abbreviate .... [shorthand]   bridge .... [shorthand]

CR

crime .... [shorthand]   credit .... [shorthand]   crown .... [shorthand]   crave .... [shorthand]

GR

grime .... [shorthand]   grown .... [shorthand]   agreed .... [shorthand]   regret .... [shorthand]

PR

product .... [shorthand]   prowl .... [shorthand]   propose .... [shorthand]   apprehend .... [shorthand]

Revision exercise 5

Unit 15 Words ending –SHUN, –SHL, –SHIP and –SHUS

Words ending -SHUN

magician .... [shorthand]   mention .... [shorthand]   occasion .... [shorthand]   ocean .... [shorthand]

oceans .... [shorthand]   fashionable .... [shorthand]   sufficient .... [shorthand]   occasional .... [shorthand]

patience .... [shorthand]   impatience .... [shorthand]   efficiency .... [shorthand]   sufficiency .... [shorthand]

Words ending -SHL

special .... [shorthand]   marshals .... [shorthand]   essentially .... [shorthand]   speciality .... [shorthand]

Words ending -SHIP

hardship .... [shorthand]   friendship .... [shorthand]   relationships .... [shorthand]   battleships .... [shorthand]

Words ending -SHUS

delicious ....   precious ....   anxious ....   cautious ....

Unit 16 T and D blends

TR/DR blend

trip ....   attract ....   reporter ....   history ....

drive ....   address ....   dark ....   moderate ....

TN/DN blend

tin ....   standing ....   retains ....   entertain ....

done ....   suddenly ....   gardens ....   redundant ....

TRN/DRN blend

train ....   returned ....   draining ....   modern ....

THR blend

other ....   mother ....   another ....   rather ....

throw ....   through ....   threat ....   thread ....

CTR blend

cater ....   collectors ....   factory ....   lecturer ....

Words beginning TRANS-

transport ....   transmit ....   transfer ....   transpire ....

Words beginning UNDER-

understand .... undermine .... undertake .... underway ....

Words ending -NESS

sweetness ....   neatness ....   sadness ....   lightness ....

Unit 17 Letter C

CM blend

camp ....   scheme ....   welcome ....   common ....

Words beginning ENCOM-/INCOM-

encompass ....   income ....   incompetent ....   incomplete ....

Words beginning RECOM-

recompense ....   recommend ....   recommendation ....

Words ending -NCE

dance ....   announced ....   balances ....   agency ....

Words ending -NCH

lunch ....   punched ....   benches ....   munching ....

CN blend

can ....   cinema ....   taken ....   inconsiderate ....

CNV blend

canvas ....   convex ....   convert ....   conventional ....

Revision exercise 6

Unit 18 Numbers, currencies, measurements, abbreviations and colloquialisms

Numbers and currencies

1	7	400	5000	2,000,000	300,000,000	5,000,000,000

¾	5%	£4	£300	€50	$20	$400	2003	1956	21st century

Measurements

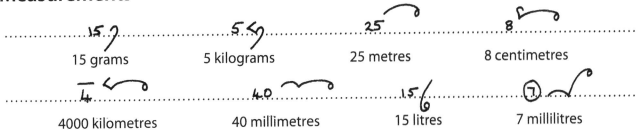

15 grams   5 kilograms   25 metres   8 centimetres

4000 kilometres   40 millimetres   15 litres   7 millilitres

Abbreviations

MP   NHS   United States of America

Days/Months

Wednesday   Saturday   January   November

Colloquialisms

I'm   I am   it's   it is

Unit 19 More word endings

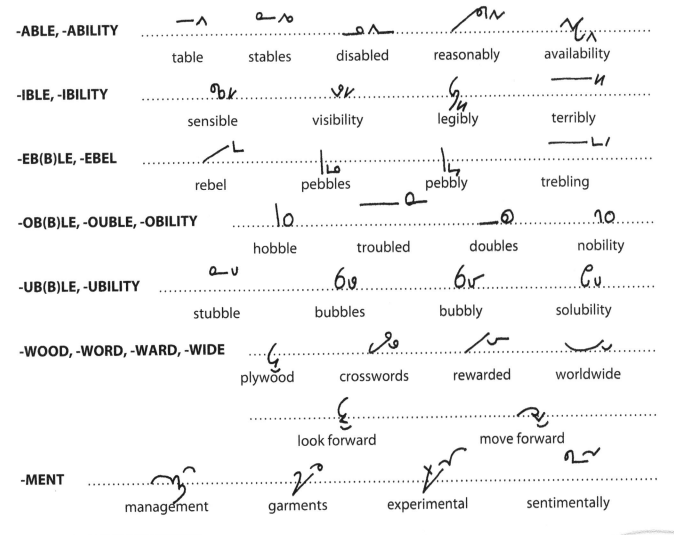

-ABLE, -ABILITY
table   stables   disabled   reasonably   availability

-IBLE, -IBILITY
sensible   visibility   legibly   terribly

-EB(B)LE, -EBEL
rebel   pebbles   pebbly   trebling

-OB(B)LE, -OUBLE, -OBILITY
hobble   troubled   doubles   nobility

-UB(B)LE, -UBILITY
stubble   bubbles   bubbly   solubility

-WOOD, -WORD, -WARD, -WIDE
plywood   crosswords   rewarded   worldwide

look forward   move forward

-MENT
management   garments   experimental   sentimentally

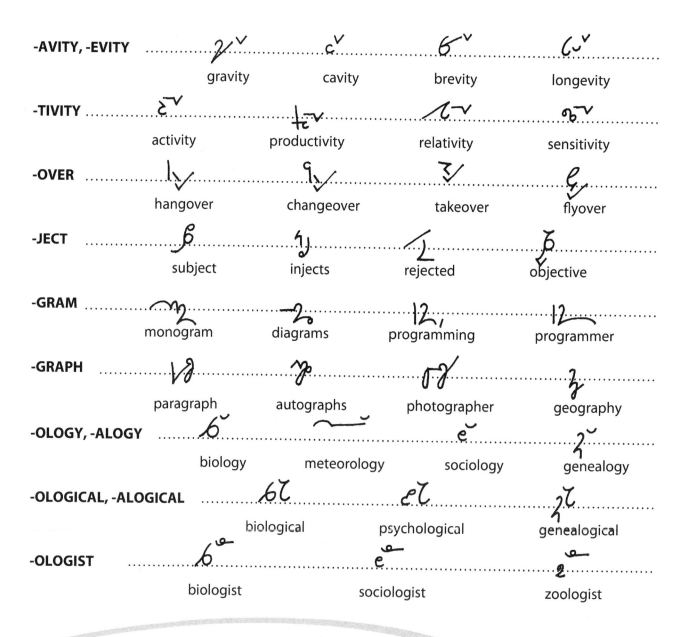

-AVITY, -EVITY	gravity	cavity	brevity	longevity
-TIVITY	activity	productivity	relativity	sensitivity
-OVER	hangover	changeover	takeover	flyover
-JECT	subject	injects	rejected	objective
-GRAM	monogram	diagrams	programming	programmer
-GRAPH	paragraph	autographs	photographer	geography
-OLOGY, -ALOGY	biology	meteorology	sociology	genealogy
-OLOGICAL, -ALOGICAL	biological	psychological	genealogical	
-OLOGIST	biologist	sociologist	zoologist	

Unit 20 More word beginnings

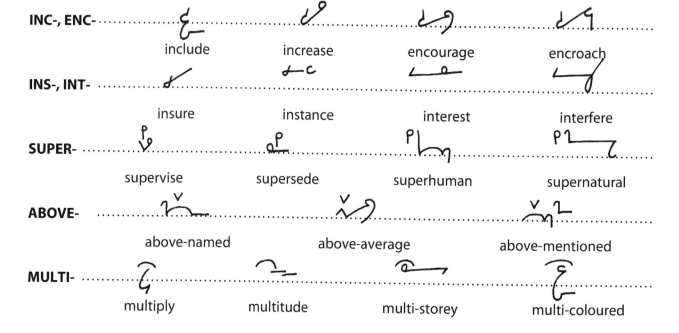

INC-, ENC-	include	increase	encourage	encroach
INS-, INT-	insure	instance	interest	interfere
SUPER-	supervise	supersede	superhuman	supernatural
ABOVE-	above-named	above-average	above-mentioned	
MULTI-	multiply	multitude	multi-storey	multi-coloured

NATION-, NON-

national nationwide nonsense non-stop

SEMI-

semi-final semi-detached semi-conscious semi-circle

ANTI-, ANTE-, ANTA-

anticipate antiquated ante-room antagonise

ELECTRI-, ELECTRO-

electrify electrocute electrode

MAGNA-, MAGNE-,
MAGNI-, MAGNO-

magnanimous magnetic magnificent magnolia

MICRO-

microphone microwave microscope microfilm

Special outlines and common words listed by unit

Unit 1

a	`
ability	∧
able/able to	∧
accident	x
after	∧
and	ʔ
are	/
at	`
be	6
been	6
began	ʔ
begin	ʔ
begun	ʔ
day	—
do	≡
electric	L
England	L
equal	ʮ
ever	ı
every	ı
evidence	v
evident	v
eye	↙

from	⌀
gentleman	ʔ
go	ʔ
have	v
he	|
I	↙
kind	<
knowledge	<
letter	(
like	<
local	(
me	⌣
of	
offence	c
once	c
page	|
pence	|
police	|
question	ʮ
south	°
southern	°
time	⌢
to	—
versus	v
very	v

village ....

we ....

you ....

your ....

Unit 3

account ....

chairman ....

company ....

each ....

etcetera ....

much ....

o'clock ....

representative ....

shall ....

such ....

that ....

the ....

they ....

what ....

which ....

with ....

within ....

without ....

Unit 4

also ....

always ....

because ....

business ....

businesses ....

hospital ....

husband ....

success ....

Unit 5

different ....

difficult ....

establish ....

immediate ....

incident ....

particular ....

residents ....

respect ....

today/to do ....

together ....

witness ....

witnesses ....

Unit 6

club ....

clubs ....

job ....

jobs ....

Unit 7

absolute	
absolutely	
city	
difficulty	
immediately	
necessary	
obvious	
obviously	
particularly	
regular	
regularly	

Unit 8

child	
employ	
guilty	
people	

Unit 9

area	
English	
equivalent	
hand	
individual	
member	
only	

opportunity	
or	
ought	
remember	

Unit 10

anything	
arrange	
enclose	
enclosed	
enclosure	
everything	
nothing	
something	

Unit 11

before	
fortunate	
frequent	
half	
inform	
manufacture	
perfect	
perfectly	
profit	
referee	
reference	
satisfactory	

successful	*el*
telephone	
therefore	
unfortunately	

Unit 12

advantage	
approximately	
disadvantage	
enthusiasm	
enthusiastic	
exchange	
exist	
expect	
experience	
however	
inexperience	
involve	
maximum	
minimum	
nevertheless	
next	
north	
several	
vandalism	

Unit 13

employer	
hour	
jury	
landlord	
mayor	
motorway	
our	
public	
remark	
tomorrow	
were	
where	
worthwhile	
world	

Unit 14

appropriate	
important	
improve	
newspaper	
permanent	
prejudice	
preliminary	
prepare	
principal	
principle	
probable	

probably	
problem	
proportion	

substantial	
their	
there	
yesterday	

Unit 15

association	
attention	
electrician	
examination	
financial	
identification	
information	
intention	
organisation	
prosecution	
qualification	
social	
society	
station	

Unit 16

alternative	
children	
extra	
extraordinary	
general	
generally	
signature	

Unit 17

circumstance	
circumstances	
committee	
communication	
community	
conference	
congratulate	
congratulations	
consequent	
convenience	
convenient	
council	
councillor	
county	
difference	
discontinue	
discount	
importance	
inconvenience	
inconvenient	
insignificant	
insurance	

NCTJ Teeline Gold Standard for Journalists

recent	....	government	....
recognise	....	impossible	....
recommend	....	technical	....
significance	....	technological	....
significant	....	technology	....
subsequent	....		

Unit 19

Unit 20

advert	....	atomic	....
advertisement	....	electricity	....
amount	....	electronic	....
department	....	super	....
develop	....	supermarket	....

Special outlines and common words listed alphabetically

a		atomic	
able		attention	
able to		be	
ability		because	
absolute		been	
absolutely		before	
accident		began	
account		begin	
advantage		begun	
advert		business	
advertisement		businesses	
after		chairman	
also		child	
alternative		children	
always		circumstance	
amount		circumstances	
and		city	
anything		club	
appropriate		clubs	
approximately		committee	
are		communication	
area		community	
arrange		company	
association		conference	
at		congratulate	

congratulations	England
consequent	English
convenience	enthusiasm
convenient	enthusiastic
council	equal
councillor	equivalent
county	establish
day	etcetera
department	ever
develop	every
difference	everything
different	evidence
difficult	evident
difficulty	examination
disadvantage	exchange
discontinue	exist
discount	expect
do	experience
each	extra
electric	extraordinary
electrician	eye
electricity	financial
electronic	fortunate
employ	frequent
employer	from
enclose	general
enclosed	generally
enclosure	gentleman

go		intention	
government		involve	
guilty		job	
half		jobs	
hand		jury	
have		kind	
he		knowledge	
hospital		landlord	
hour		letter	
however		like	
husband		local	
I		manufacture	
identification		maximum	
immediate		mayor	
immediately		me	
importance		member	
important		minimum	
impossible		motorway	
improve		much	
incident		necessary	
inconvenience		nevertheless	
inconvenient		next	
individual		newspaper	
inexperience		north	
inform		nothing	
information		o'clock	
insignificant		obvious	
insurance		obviously	

of		prosecution	
offence		public	
once		qualification	
only		question	
opportunity		recent	
or		recognise	
organisation		recommend	
ought		referee	
our		reference	
page		regular	
particular		regularly	
particularly		remark	
pence		remember	
people		representative	
perfect		residents	
perfectly		respect	
permanent		satisfactory	
police		several	
prejudice		shall	
preliminary		signature	
prepare		significance	
principal		significant	
principle		social	
probable		society	
probably		something	
problem		south	
profit		southern	
proportion		station	

subsequent	....	tomorrow	....
substantial	....	unfortunately	....
success	....	vandalism	....
successful	....	versus	....
such	....	very	....
super	....	village	....
supermarket	....	we	....
technical	....	were	....
technological	....	what	....
technology	....	where	....
telephone	....	which	....
that	....	worthwhile	....
the	....	with	....
their	....	within	....
there	....	without	....
therefore	....	witness	....
they	....	witnesses	....
time	....	world	....
to	....	yesterday	....
today/to do	....	you	....
together	....	your	....

Distinguishing outlines

Unit 4

amaze		amuse	
his		has	
perhaps		purpose	
this		these	those

Unit 7

behind	beyond
year old	years old
years ago	years of age

Unit 8

last	least
man	men
simple	sample
woman	women

Unit 9

ease	use
easy	easier
easily	usually

Unit 11

firm .... *(outline)* .... form .... *(outline)* .... farm .... *(outline)* ....

Unit 12

exceed .... *(outline)* .... exact .... *(outline)* ....

lovely .... *(outline)* .... lively .... *(outline)* ....

now .... *(outline)* .... new/knew .... *(outline)* .... no/number/know .... *(outline)* ....

Unit 13

smaller .... *(outline)* .... similar .... *(outline)* ....

Unit 14

press .... *(outline)* .... papers .... *(outline)* ....

Unit 15

specialist .... *(outline)* .... specialised .... *(outline)* ....

Unit 16

feature .... *(outline)* .... future .... *(outline)* ....

farther .... *(outline)* .... further .... *(outline)* ....

Unit 17

come .... *(outline)* .... came .... *(outline)* ....

become .... *(outline)* .... became .... *(outline)* ....

NCTJ Teeline Gold Standard for Journalists

Unit 19

sociology ....ĕ............   psychology ....ĕ............

Word groupings

Unit 6

and the	
are you	
are you able to	
as soon as	
as soon as possible	
at the	
at the same time	
by the	
could be	
do you	
from the	
has been	
he is able to	
I am able to	
I am sure	
I have been	
I must	
I shall	
I will have	
I would	
I would like	
if the	
in fact	

is the	
it is	
it would	
may be	
of course	
of the	
that his	
that the	
that these	
that this	
that those	
that was	
that was a	
the fact that	
the facts	
these facts	
they are	
they would	
to be	
to say	
to see	
to the	
we are	
we are able to	
we have	

we have been	....	men and women	....
we have the	....	men or women	....
we shall	....	not guilty	....
we should have	....	some facilities	....
we will	....	the facility	....
we would	....	we are pleased	....
will be	....	you will be pleased	....
with the	....		
would be	....		
would have	....		
would we	....		
would we be able to	....		
would you	....		
you are	....		
you do	....		
you have	....		
you will	....		
you would	....		

Unit 9

after all	....
no doubt	....
on the other hand	....
over and done with	....
over and over	....
over and over again	....
over that	....
over the	....
over this	....

Unit 8

a lot of	....
as a result	....
hospital facilities	....
I am pleased	....
it is my pleasure	....
ladies and gentlemen	....
man and woman	....
man or woman	....

Unit 10

all things	....
anything else	....
do you think	....
doing the	....
everything else	....
good thing	....
having the	....
his thanks	....

I think		past few years	
making the		so far as	
many thanks		telephone call	
many things		telephone number	
most things		with reference to	
needing the			
nothing else			
something else			

Unit 12

chief executive	
for example	
in the	
in the north	
in these days	
in those days	
they have	
upside down	

taking the

thank you

thank you for your

these things

they thanked

they think

vote of thanks

we are thinking

we enclose

we thank

we think

your thanks

Unit 13

all over the city	
all over the place	
all over the town	
all over the world	
all parts of the world	
in our	
in our opinion	
ladies and gentlemen of the jury	
larger and larger	
members of the jury	

Unit 11

as far as	
first of all	
for ever and ever	
for the	
from time to time	
last few weeks	

members of the public		local authorities	
more and more		more than	
more or less		name and address	
Mr and Mrs		names and addresses	
my opinion		rather than	
our opinion		that there/their	
smaller and smaller		the authority	
sum of money		there has been	
sums of money		whether or not	
this morning		your authority	
your opinion			

Unit 14

car park	
good deal	
great deal	
it is important	
most important	

Unit 16

as a matter of fact	
better than	
during their	
greater than	
health authority	
in order that	
in order to	
less than	

Appendix 4

Unit 17

at once	
at the end	
at the end of the day	
at the middle	
borough council	
by the middle	
Chamber of Commerce	
circumstantial evidence	
city council	
come to the conclusion	
council tax	
county council	
district council	
for instance	
from the centre	
from the end	

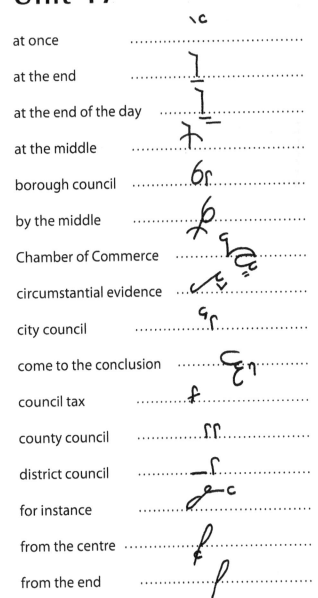

from the middle	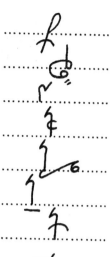
House of Commons	
I can	
in the centre	
in the circumstances	
in the end	
in the middle	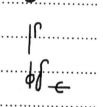
income tax	
leisure centre	
parish council	
press conference	
town centre	
town council	
we can	
you can	

point of view	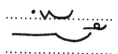
there were thousands of	

Unit 19

go forward	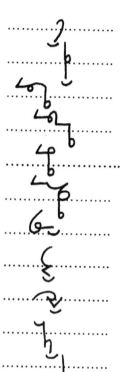
hospital ward	
it is impossible	
it is not possible	
it is possible	
it will be possible	
last word	
look forward	
move forward	
open wide	
put forward	

Unit 18

come straight to the point	
many hundreds of	
on the spot	

Unit 20

anti-social behaviour	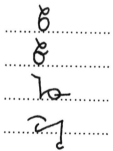
anti-social behaviour order	
at home and abroad	
multi-storey car park	